MUSIC CLUBS, FESTIVALS & CONCERTS

MUSIC CLUBS, FESTIVALS & CONCERTS
and How to Organize Them

by

PHYL DUTTON

GRESHAM BOOKS

First published in 1981 by

GRESHAM BOOKS LTD
THE GRESHAM PRESS
OLD WOKING, SURREY
ENGLAND

ISBN 0 905418 86 7

Printed and bound in Great Britain by
STAPLES PRINTERS ST ALBANS at the Priory Press

Contents

APPENDICES

Foreword

It is with unqualified enthusiasm that I recommend this book of information to prospective secretaries or anyone connected with running music clubs either established or in course of foundation or with running local festivals or single concerts.

So many things are entailed in their success both from the audience point of view and from that of the performers. For the latter, music clubs often provide their first professional opportunity to perform before an audience as well as being the mainstay of much of their careers. For the former, music clubs are the essential ingredient for a musical community, whether promoting chamber music in a large city where there is already a Symphony Orchestra or in a small village which desperately needs an outlet for music lovers. They provide enjoyment, enhance the artistic life of the community and offer relaxation to those under stress, as do festivals and single concerts.

This book demonstrates a sympathetic understanding of the problems of promoter and performer, each of whom is dependent on the other, and is the A.B.C. of creating and sustaining a successful music club and running a successful festival or concert. It will be of invaluable help to everyone connected with these enterprises which give so much to the community and mean so much to the profession and in so doing will make a valuable contribution towards keeping the professional performance of music alive.

DAME ISOBEL BAILLIE, DBE

Acknowledgements

For help, encouragement, advice, information or allowing me to quote them, my very great thanks to: Dame Isobel Baillie, DBE, Sir Charles Groves, CBE, John Lill, Ian Wallace, Wilfrid Van Wyck, Susan Alcock and Pamela Bowden (Gen. Sec. and Assistant Administrator ISM), John Crisp (Gen. Sec. NFMS), Ken Blakeley (Arts Council Liaison Officer to the NFMS), Helen Fraser (Assistant Music Officer SAC), Anthony Friese Greene (BBC), Keith Griffin (Welsh Arts Council), D. Llion Williams (Director, N. Wales Arts Association), D. J. Mulholland (Arts Council of Northern Ireland), Anthony Woodcock (Music Officer SEAA), A. G. Bell (Senior Environmental Health Officer, Woking Borough Council), Jonson Dyer (Man. Dir. Peters Editions Ltd., for Performing Right information), Stanley Weedon and Shirley Lupton (founder and secretary of the Three Rivers Music Society); the officers of the many music clubs who so willingly supplied me with examples of programmes and information; the many young, maturing and established musicians for their stories, information and encouragement; Francis Clarke for his photographs; my colleagues ex- and present on Woking Music Club's Committee for their interest and encouragement; my husband, family, sister and friends for their encouragement and so understandingly putting up with my unsociability during the research and writing of this guide.

Abbreviations

GLAA	Greater London Arts Association
ISM	Incorporated Society of Musicians
NFMS	National Federation of Music Societies
RAA	Regional Arts Association
RAM	Royal Academy of Music
RCM	Royal College of Music
SAC	Scottish Arts Council
SEAA	South East Arts Association
WAC	Welsh Arts Council
WAMF	Welsh Amateur Music Federation
WRAA	Welsh Regional Arts Association
YML	Young Musicians' Liaison

Introduction

During the present difficult times of financial cut-back, audience short-fall and the consequent threat to the future of professional music-making, the need for the utmost ingenuity and efficiency in running amateur concert-promoting organizations, especially music clubs, is now a matter of extreme urgency. I am convinced that amateur promoters can do more than anyone else to safeguard and keep professional music-making alive and forging ahead in the face of adversity. Amateur concert-promoting is a labour of love both to your community and the profession, neither of whom can do without the other. By bringing the joy of such 'in the flesh' performances to your neighbourhood you give many people their only chance of such experiences, you introduce others to a lifelong love and interest they might otherwise never have had, and give people the opportunity to improve their musical knowledge, experience and appreciation.

At the same time you serve the music profession in no small way. For its members rely on the amateur promoters, and music clubs in particular, for their bread and butter and for career building purposes. You, in turn, derive a great sense of privilege from being involved in such a worthwhile service.

However, though termed 'amateur' there must be nothing amateurish about the forming or running of your organization. Be it a music club, a festival, an occasional-concert-promoting body or an amateur orchestral or choral society promoting its own concerts, it must be formed and run as efficiently and practically as possible and function to the best effect by being fully aware of and understanding *all* its roles, learning how best to play them and acting accordingly.

It is the object of this book to provide the information to inspire and help the prospective or established amateur promoter. The size and make-up of a locality's population, its geographical location and terrain and the local financial climate determine the size of clubs and audiences. But only up to a point, for this should be looked on as a challenge because there is always room for improvement, however limiting these factors: improvement which, if your heart is truly in your project and you are prepared to work all out for it, can be achieved, as my own experience has taught me.

I have tried to make this book a mine of positive, ordered information about everything to do with the forming, running and function of all types of amateur concert-promoting organizations including schools. It is based on my experiences and observations while working for Woking Music Club as PRO cum Concert Secretary and Manager, running a Festival and single concerts including assisting with London ones. I have also drawn on those of audiences, of other clubs, promoters (amateur and professional), agents, orchestral managements and artists with whom I have necessarily been in contact.

I do not pretend that my book can take the hard work out of such projects. Nothing can if you are to make a first-class job of it. But it may simplify matters by saving time and delay, because you will be able to avoid some of the pitfalls. I hope it will help to put new life into failing clubs and to encourage the proliferation of new clubs, festivals and concerts; I hope also it will be a very real contribution towards helping to solve at least some of the problems of the music world in its widest sense: that is of the artists, and those on whom they depend, namely amateur and professional promoters, agents, orchestral managements, choral societies and so on.

Your ambition may be to promote one festival or concert, found a club, run one more successfully or give one the kiss of life. Mine is to see this happen wherever needed, to see greater understanding of professional musicians and to see more and more people coming together to enjoy their music making.

Founding and running Amateur Concert-promoting Clubs, Festivals and Single Concerts

1. THE RIGHT APPROACH: PERSONAL AND PRACTICAL

If a job is to be well done you must have the right tools and know how to use them. The two vital tools of the amateur festival and concert promoter or club organizer are *the personal approach* and *the practical approach*. You will make little headway without them.

1. *The personal approach* supplies that human element so necessary to running anything local. It makes the difference between a constantly growing, go-ahead project and one that just limps along or founders. It brings life and meaning to your club, festival or concert both for the audience and members and for the administration. For the audience and members it provides the warm, welcoming factor which sweeps aside the barriers of what many consider to be tight-knit, high-brow circles and destroys the reputation for snobbishness which clubs—sometimes still not without reason—have earned, which does literally frighten people away. On the administrative side it is the lubrication for smooth, harmonious running, the key to good liaison and happy working relationships. It secures as nothing else will, a far greater chance of winning understanding, interested and often enthusiastic help from all you deal with and is especially valuable when seeking sponsors, guarantors, donations and so on. It is the *only* effective way of building up good will. Without it, no matter how efficient and businesslike you are, you will make a stony path for yourselves.

The personal approach, as I see it, is to tackle whatever you do in a personal way from a personal angle. It is *not* taking a concert preview in person to a local paper and just leaving it for someone to take to the appropriate editor or reporter. It *is* asking to see that person, discussing the preview with him or if you can't see him, writing a friendly note pointing out the essentials. It is *not* putting a new member's membership card and literature through the letterbox but handing it over in person, introducing yourself and welcoming him or her to the club.

The personal approach works for several reasons. Practically, you are at an

1

immediate advantage if talking rather than writing to someone. When talking you will know after the first few words how to continue to the best effect. The personal approach works because you can see and hear things for yourself and act accordingly. Psychologically it works because generally speaking, though few admit it, people are flattered when appealed to personally. The more understanding you give them, the greater the inner glow and response in becoming as zealous as you in pursuit of the project's success. Always use the personal approach. Never phone if you can see someone. Never write if you can phone. Make people feel they matter. Infect them with your enthusiasm. Involve them. The personal approach is the PRO's greatest tool. It *is* Public Relations (see page 13).

2. *The practical approach* is your other great aid and ally, for there must be nothing haphazard in your approach to the planning and carrying through of your project or, no matter how good your personal approach or purposeful your committee, you will head for trouble. Lose no time in making sure that your project is feasible before going ahead (see Check List, Appendix 5), in planning programmes, caring for artists, etc. Practically, all matters must be considered in relation to one another and actions planned accordingly. A wall planner is a great help in working everything out: at a glance you can see when your deadlines are for getting copy to the printer or the press, when posters must go up and the umpteen other things that must be attended to and which, if forgotten, can lose goodwill, members and ticket sales. The practical approach is as vital and essential as the personal approach and most necessary when forming a committee.

2. THE COMMITTEE

Just as you must have the right tools for the job so you must have the right people for it. Your committee should be set up with great care. Your aim is to form a purposeful group which will leave no doubt as to its ability and intention to work as a team to do the job it is set up to do.

Ideally, every one of its members should be prepared to work hard for it. Nothing is worse than having a committee in which only a couple of its members are landed with all the work. Yet this does happen. Jobs are not done when they should be. People are not keen to put themselves out. In desperation the secretary or some other committee member takes on more and more.

Why should this happen? Because, for one reason or another the wrong people are asked on to a committee: perhaps because it is felt that they would be hurt if not asked; perhaps because they have managed to inveigle themselves on, simply for the kudos they hope to gain but with no idea of what is entailed. Or perhaps, the wrong people are there because, it being a musical project, the committee has been formed almost entirely of people connected with music but with no regard as to whether they would either have the time or ability to cope with matters other than music; or again, because it is not realised at the time that some committee members will be physically incapable of the hard work necessary at times. So, do give very careful thought as to the make-up of your committee. It must be well balanced. Although it is a musical project this does not mean that it should be loaded with musicians or music teachers. Their job, which is chiefly to advise on choice of artists and programme content and to write programme notes, is only part of all that must be done. Moreover, they are very busy people unable to spare the large amount of time required.

Good team work is essential for smooth running. Members should be capable of carrying out their tasks on time; of anticipating where hold-ups may occur and coping accordingly; of giving a hand without having to be asked; of seeing what needs to be done and doing it; of knowing when or when not to come back to the chairman or treasurer before making a decision. They should be conscientious, dependable, hard-working and prepared to turn their hands to most things. My mention of physical capability was no idle remark. This is something not always taken into consideration yet most important if you don't wish to find the brunt of the work having to be done by only a few. Remember that there is plenty of standing to be done; staging may have to be shifted, chairs moved, food prepared and so on; there are times when you never seem to stop, when you will need all the stamina you can muster. So that the more of you whose backs, joints and feet are in good working order the better.

All members of a committee should have their hearts in the project, and if possible be blessed with the gift of the gab and the crusading spirit. It is the duty of a committee to spread the word. Its responsibility is to make as great a success of your project as possible. One of the surest ways of doing this is by word of mouth. When approaching possible committee members *do* sound them out before actually inviting them on. If you cannot infect them with your own enthusiasm there is no point in going further. But, whatever you do, put them in the picture before letting them accept. Make sure that they know what they could be letting themselves in for—not only the special job you have in mind for them but the others they will have to do at times such as ticket selling, poster or leaflet distribution, manning the box office, stewarding and so on. Also ensure that they will be able to spare the time which can be considerable for some of the jobs, and that they really will be available when most needed. You will need to be bold and courageous in your search for an as ideal a committee as you can find. You cannot afford to jeopardise the success of your venture for the sake of not upsetting people. Your aim

3

must be to run your project to the best possible effect with as few headaches as possible which means no passengers on the committee. Bear this constantly in mind and don't be deterred, because whether your project stands or falls will rest entirely on your choice of committee.

Make-up of the committee is much the same whether for running a club, festival or concert. It is vital that one member should be the king pin, all-seeing, far-seeing and capable of organizing and correlating everything so that it all falls together smoothly piece by piece. It is only the clubs and organizations with such a one which really succeed.

The size of your committee will depend on the number of jobs to be done: publicity and public relations can be done by one person and can even be merged with concert management; a president could also be the chairman; a chairman could be and often is the Federal Representative (NFMS affiliated clubs) or the committee secretary and so on. Remember that an Hon. Auditor is needed if you intend to affiliate with the NFMS (clubs), apply for grant aid from your RAA/WRAA/the SAC or become a registered or recognized charity.

3. FINANCE

TREASURER

Your treasurer should be a person of figures—an accountant or experienced staff member of a bank, building society or insurance company branch etc.— able to weigh up situations, make the right decisions and extract the best terms, especially when dealing with hall managements or local authorities. Preferably he or she should be available during weekdays to avoid the necessity of delegating bank visits to another committee member. Indeed, a festival treasurer should only be appointed on the understanding that he or she will be available throughout the vital run-up to and during the festival itself.

The treasurer will be responsible for doing all or some of the following according to the type of your project:

(a) opening a current account at the bank in the name of your organization and arranging for cheques to be signed by him or herself and countersigned by one of two other committee members (as available) who shall be appointed as signatories by the committee;

(b) opening a deposit account so that funds in hand can earn their keep until needed. Registered or recognized charities are exempt from income tax on interest;

(c) providing a budget for your committee's guidance;

(d) ensuring that expenditure does not exceed income. He or she must always be consulted if you find you cannot keep within the budget stipulations;

(e) keeping the committee regularly informed on the state of the finances;
(f) collecting subscriptions, ticket sales' receipts and any other income;
(g) arranging for public liability and keyboard insurances (if hiring);
(h) payment of performing right fees where necessary or of the NFMS tariff covering these fees if NFMS affiliated;
(i) payment of NFMS/RAA/WRAA/WAMF subscriptions as applicable;
(j) applying as appropriate for guarantees or grant aid to the NFMS/WAMF/RAAs/SAC;
(k) instigating the raising of funds to cover special objectives;
(l) dealing with covenanting;
(m) paying all accounts after the committee's sanction;
(n) keeping proper accounts which must be presented clearly and simply in the form of a Financial Statement at the end of your organization's financial year, festival or concert;
(o) arranging for the auditing of accounts if NFMS affiliated or receiving aid from RAAs/WAMF/SAC or if required by your constitution.

Before there are any returns, it may be possible for:
(a) the secretary and PRO to carry their expenses for a while;
(b) the committee to contribute a substantial, recoverable float;
(c) one of the committee to provide a substantial, recoverable float. In fact this is often done by the founder or instigator of a project;
(d) other interested persons to supply a recoverable float.

Failing the above, seek donations or hold fund-raising events. You are not looking for vast amounts, but just enough to cover the initial expenses until the returns start to come in, which will be as soon as you have something to tell people. You can then begin seeking sponsors, guarantors and further donations; you can also start a patrons scheme. Some people fancy having their names on a patrons' list, the donation permitting this (which must be made by a certain time) being thought worth it for that alone. But, add such privileges as special advance priority booking, special subscription rates and you can be sure of funds coming in. However, few people will want to take advantage of such schemes unless they know what the programmes are, and this information cannot be given until your plans are confirmed and artists booked, which cannot be done until you know approximately what you can afford in fees.

PROVISIONAL BUDGET

One of your treasurer's first jobs is to work out a provisional budget showing roughly how much there will be to spend on artists after *all* incidental

5

expenses have been accounted for. Estimated expenses can then be offset against estimated income and the balance used for artists' fees. Expenses and sources of income will vary according to the type of project but will include (as appropriate) all or some of the following:

Expenses
(a) administration expenses which include: postage, stationery, materials for exhibitions, telephone, committee members' expenses (see note below);
(b) hire of venue/s;
(c) printing and/or duplicating;
(d) hire of piano, its insurance *or* cost of moving, tuning and insuring a borrowed piano *or* the tuning of a resident piano;
(e) ditto for harpsichord or other keyboard instruments;
(f) public liability and employers' insurance (this can be done via the NFMS if affiliated);
(g) Music, Singing and Dancing Licence (where needed);
(h) NFMS subscription and other NFMS expenses as appropriate;
(i) expenses or assistance with same of delegate attending NFMS conference or regional meetings (optional);
(j) RAA/WRAA subscription;
(k) expenses to attend RAA/WRAA general meetings, symposia etc. (optional);
(l) performing right fees;
(m) hospitality for artists if necessary;
(n) advertising, rent of poster sites, leaflet delivery with papers etc;
(o) hire of lighting equipment if needed and not borrowed;
(p) hire of staging if needed and not borrowed;
(q) cost of transporting staging if borrowed;
(r) any other expenses peculiar to your particular project.

NOTE It is important not to underestimate the committee's expenses especially those of your king-pin-cum-general organizer, which, if the project is to succeed, must be fairly heavy, particularly for phone and petrol. In my opinion there should also be an annual honorarium where such a person puts in many, many hours, in recognition of their devotion. Indeed, there are several music clubs already doing this because they know that without their king-pin the club would fade.

Sources of Income
(a) subscriptions;
(b) sale of season tickets;
(c) sale of single tickets;

(d) sale of concert programmes;
(e) sale of festival programme brochures;
(f) sale of advertising space;
(g) sale of refreshments;
(h) donations;
(i) fund-raising events;
(j) sponsorship and/or guarantees;
(k) grant aid and/or guarantees from RAA/WRAA/WAMF/SAC (see Appendix 2);
(l) guarantees and other benefits from the NFMS (see Appendix 1);
(m) grants from voluntary grant-making trusts (see below);
(n) grants/subsidies/guarantees from local authorities or education authorities;
(o) interest on deposited monies;
(p) proceeds from raffles, bring-and-buy stalls etc.

FUND RAISING

1. *The NFMS, English and Welsh RAAs/WAMF/SAC.* Study the appropriate information (Appendices 1 and 2) so that you can then plan to fulfill the conditions most beneficial to your organization.

2. *Local authorities* including those neighbouring your own (if it can be shown that a fair proportion of your audiences are drawn from their areas) may be able to make grants, guarantees or subsidies.

3. *Local education authorities* may be able to provide aid for events of educational value.

4. *Parish or parochial church councils* may help with donations, guarantees, or lend their churches or halls especially for festivals.

5. *Trusts.* There are over 200 voluntary grant-making bodies in England and Wales from some of which you may be able to obtain aid. But as the terms of reference of most charitable bodies preclude them from considering applications for grants or donations from any but registered or recognized charities you must become one if you are not already. Details of these grant-making bodies are in the Directory of Grant-making Trusts to be found in main Public Libraries which gives information on the resources available and how to apply for them. Also available is a leaflet 'Presenting your Case' giving guidance on how to apply to trusts from the Charities Aid Foundation, 48 Penbury Rd., Tonbridge, Kent TN9 2JD. (See Appendices 1 and 2).

6. *Covenanting.* Your organization must be registered or recognized as a charity to benefit in this way.

7. *Sponsoring.* Fortunately a growing number of concerns are making it their policy to sponsor the promotion of music in one form or another. Many companies may require a 'return service' which can include naming the concert or event after the sponsors; a specially designed programme cover; giving the sponsorship the widest possible publicity; special acknowledgement in the concert programme; complimentary tickets for the sponsor, sponsor's personnel and friends; arranging for the sponsor to meet the artists, committee, and local dignitaries after the concert; photographs of sponsors with artists; ensuring that press previews and reviews acknowledge the sponsorship; supplying sponsors with copies of *all* printed publicity.

Unless you know that a particular concern has had a bad year or that sponsoring is not their policy, try everyone. Keep up to date with the goings on in the national or local commercial world. Although major companies tend to sponsor big events, what you have to offer may just appeal to them. Sometimes a firm may be looking for a prestigious way of integrating into a new community to which they have recently re-located. Some know just what they want to sponsor, others want ideas. One may wish to sponsor the commission of a new work and its premier; another to bring great artists, far beyond your means, to the district; another to pay all or part of the costs of an orchestra and so on.

For advice on organizations with a serious 'package' to offer, you could apply to the Association of Business Sponsorship of the Arts (ABSA) at 12 Abbey Churchyard, Bath BA1 1LY. Tel: (0225) 63762. This is not a fund-raising or grant-giving organization but provides a service for sponsors by seeking events for them and not sponsors for events, and it is not an agency.

8. *Fund Raising by yourselves.* This can be done in many ways from holding garden or lunch parties to sponsored walks; from bring-and-buy sales to running a market stall. The Hereward Singers (NFMS) do this with such success that they also take stalls at agricultural shows. One music society keeps a collecting box on the bar of their 'local' with excellent results. Form a fund-raising sub-committee to co-ordinate all ideas.

9. *Sale of advertising space* on programme covers, or inserted in concert programmes, seasonal programme brochures and festival brochures can be used to offset or even cover the cost of printing.

NOTE The smaller the advertisement space the more you should charge in proportion. First find out the cost of printing; then work out a charge for each sized space so that whatever permutation of spaces you sell you will not only cover the cost but make a profit.

10. *Sale of Concert Programmes or Festival Brochures* should also produce a profit or at least cover the cost of their duplication or printing. A considerable saving can be made here if you can do your own duplicating, or find someone willing to do it free for you.

TICKET PRICING

Single Tickets for Concerts or for each Festival Concert. Be canny. People want value for money. Price too low and they may suspect that the concert or artists are inferior. Price too high and you may price yourselves out of business.

Special Sales Promotion Rates for single tickets or festival season tickets. If offering these, calculate them so that you will not lose if the greater part of your sales is made in this way.

Clubs' subscriptions serial tickets, non-member single tickets. See NFMS guidelines, (Appendix 1) which could apply equally to non-affiliated clubs. There should be a reassessment of these rates each year rather than trying to hold prices.

Other pricing points to consider:
1. Though expensive, big names sell more tickets for which, within reason, you can charge more. Here the deciding factor is seating capacity. If it is so small as to make pricing prohibitively high, then forget it unless you can find a sponsor or some other means of covering part of the fee so that you can price reasonably.
2. Don't overprice charity concerts, for, though prepared to pay more for such concerts, people still have their limits.
3. The type of venue can also influence pricing: people are prepared to pay more for concerts in unique or historic or really well appointed venues.
4. For small venues you may have to limit the numbers of concessionary OAP or Junior tickets.

ARTISTS' FEES

Artists' fees vary according to the artist's drawing power. Many artists charge VAT or may do so by the time they appear for you. Be on the safe side and *always* allow for this and possible travelling expenses. Artists domiciled abroad do not charge VAT.

Amateur orchestras or choirs do not come free! Usually there are professional orchestral stiffeners, the conductor, possibly professional soloists, the travelling expenses of whom and of some amateurs have to be paid. Audiences do not expect to have to pay as much for amateur or semi-professional concerts as for all professional ones. If the artist is engaged via an agent, the agent will invoice you a day or two before or after the concert. Payment should be made as soon after the concert as possible. Alternatively, artists may give you an invoice on the day; if they are diffident about bringing the matter up you should raise it. In any case, they should receive their cheque directly after the concert, or they may prefer to invoice you a day or two after the concert, in which case settle up at once.

Obviously, there must be guesswork with a Provisional Budget. Even a successful club can never be sure of membership from season to season let alone non-member ticket sales. There are many hazards in concert promoting. You may not land the sponsorship you had hoped for; what seemed an attractive concert or series of concerts may not seem so to others; flu epidemics or extremes of weather may pull audiences right down; a nearby event or riveting TV programme may clash with yours; or an adventurous concert may make larger losses than allowed for. Never, therefore, base your calculations on the supposition that concerts will sell out or your subscription list fill.

4. THE CONCERT VENUE

Ideally a concert venue should have good acoustics; comfortable seating which is either stepped on a raked floor, or on a level floor with a high platform; possibly a balcony, gallery or tiers; a first rate concert-grand piano; and attractive decor. It should be economically viable and neither too large nor too small for the purposes in hand. It should hold a 'Music Singing and Dancing Licence' (if required) or be easily adapted to be so licensed (see page 27). There should be adequate but *silent* heating, ventilation and lighting (fluorescent tubes can set up a loud hum); warm comfortable dressing rooms for the artists; a greenroom where people can meet the artists; facilities for serving refreshments; a bar; good cloakrooms; box-office facilities; its own or good parking nearby. So much for the dream!

What you are far more likely to have to cope with is a venue with only a few of these good points. It may be a cathedral, church, theatre, stately home, art gallery, public library; a village, school, church, town, civic, university, college or other institution hall or a private drawing room; but whatever it is, especially if you use it regularly, you owe it to both the performers and audiences to do your utmost to improve or rectify at least the shortcomings of the auditorium so that music can be performed and heard in as ideal conditions as possible.

By and large a lot can be done. It will take determination, a refusal to be baulked, and, possibly a combined effort by all local promoting and performing organizations using the same venue. Money must be raised if considerable expense is involved, and where necessary, you must persuade the powers that be of the importance of such improvements, not just for the performers and audiences but for themselves, as enhanced facilities lead to enhanced prestige, larger attendances and so greater takings. So let us see what can be done:

1. *Acoustic Problems.* Broadly speaking, an auditorium is acoustically good for music if it has a resonance or echo when empty which does not entirely disappear when full. Most musicians call this 'brightness' and prefer an auditorium to err a little on the bright rather than the 'dry' or 'dead' side. That is when sound is soaked up by carpeting, upholstery, heavy drapes, curtains or sound absorbent finishes to walls, ceilings or floors, as well as by the audience; all this makes it difficult for performers to judge balance, projection and indeed, to 'get across', and the audience also suffers by not hearing the music at its best. Too much brightness in venues almost entirely devoid of absorbent material, such as cathedrals, churches, school halls and so on, can also cause problems, for then the notes rebound and echo to and fro, colliding and blurring.

It may not be possible to cure your venue's acoustic defects completely: there are too many indeterminate factors, including size of audience. But you will be able to improve them, though it may take a certain amount of trial and error.

(a) *In overbright auditoriums* resonance can be damped with curtaining, carpeting or something to prevent the sound from rebounding between walls or from roof to floor, such as the portable acoustic shell used in the church by the St. Mary's (Primrose Hill) Music Club. Made on professional advice, it prevents the notes from the performers, who stand within its arc, from soaring and reverberating and directs them towards the audience.

(b) *In 'dry' auditoriums* the soaking up effect can be diminished by removing non-permanent carpeting, drapes or upholstered seats not in use. Stage drapes or curtains and window curtains can be pulled right back. It may be possible to use acoustic resonating boards to throw sound into the auditorium, a method used to good effect in the large marquee used for concerts at the Festival of English Music at Bracknell. Made from thick hardboard (for the deep notes), covered in melamine (for the high notes), in four leaves which could be folded for storing, this most useful contrivance cost under £100 to construct.

11

If matters are not improved enough with the above methods seek professional advice. A university or technical college with an acoustics section to its physics faculty or department may, subject to approval, be able to arrange (as Surrey University did for Woking Music Club) for an acoustics' survey to be carried out in the hall as a student project under supervision, at little or no cost, and remedies recommended, but with no guarantee that they will work. The implementation of the recommendations can then be discussed with the hall or venue management and action taken accordingly.

2. *Noisy heating and ventilation* is a fault in many new so-called all-purpose halls (did no one remember music?). The only answer here is to have both culprits switched off before the start of concerts. Audience body heat will maintain and even increase the temperature thereafter.

3. *Noisy fluorescent lighting* can be cured electronically; otherwise, provided that there are alternative lights, however dim, switch off the strip lights during the performance. Though it may be difficult to read programmes this is infinitely preferable to the distracting hum which also upsets the musician's ear.

4. *Inadequate heating* can be a problem especially in churches or cathedrals. If it is impossible to improve the heating during the winter it is better to hold your concerts during the warmer months. You cannot expect superb performances or large audiences in venues where the breath hangs on the air. Remember too that venues should be comfortably warm for rehearsals.

5. *Platforms unable to take the weight of concert-grand pianos* (see page 26).

6. *Inadequate or non-existent platforms.* It is important that the whole audience should have a good view of the performers. Every effort should be made to raise low platforms where seating is not raked or tiered, or to provide staging if none exists. Staging can be hired (expensive), borrowed, (when its transport must be paid for), or made as a once and for all expense, which could be a joint effort between other societies. Choral societies in England and Scotland affiliated to the NFMS may obtain a loan on easy terms for the purchase or construction of staging.

7. *Dowdy, unattractive venues* are uninspiring to artists and audiences, concerts being that much more enjoyed and much better performed in pleasant surroundings. Flower or foliage decoration on the platform and in the foyer or entrance hall do more than anything to lift the gloom and transform the atmosphere into one of welcome and uplift. Local authorities should be able to bedeck their halls with plants from their park greenhouses. Liaise with

them about this. Or it may be possible to have an arrangement with a florist or garden centre to provide pot plants free, as an advertisement, to be returned after the concert. Or perhaps your local Floral Arrangement Society might care to demonstrate their art at your concerts.

8. *Inadequate dressing rooms.* These can be claustrophobically small, comfortless and not very warm. Certainly not places where artists can rest if they prefer to be on their own between rehearsal and concert. In such circumstances make every effort to obtain the use of other rooms where you can supply a sun-lounger, refreshment and if necessary extra heating (see also page 35).

9. *Bar facilities.* If there is no bar at your venue do your best to arrange for one. Temporary Bar Licences are issued by the Licensing Justices' Clerk (listed under 'Courts' in the telephone directory). The bar must be run by a professional bar tender. A bar is an attraction in itself especially where clubs are concerned for it helps to create an intimate atmosphere.

10. *Other refreshments.* Always arrange for coffee or soft drinks during the interval. Not everyone wants to use a bar. If, apart from power points, there are no other facilities then you should supply an urn and everything else necessary, provided the venue management agrees.

It is vital that you do all that you can to make your venue as comfortable, attractive, efficient and welcoming as possible. Ensure that everything about the various parts of the venue looks well kempt, including the piano. Finger marks on this can be seen right at the back of a hall let alone at the front. Attention to such details will enhance your reputation.

5. PUBLICITY AND PUBLIC RELATIONS

These are the means used to acquaint people with the various lures that you have devised to entice them to snap up your offers and join your club, take out season tickets, attend your festival or buy concert tickets etc. Without them, no matter how tempting those lures, halls will not fill nor organizations flourish. Publicity in the broadest sense is the advertising, the making known to the public of an organization's products and promotions—in this context, concerts, festivals or music clubs. *Public Relations (PR)* is a form of publicity which is used continuously for the good of an organization while at the same time assisting its promotions. The Institute of Public Relations defines its practise as the 'the deliberate, planned and sustained effort to establish and maintain mutual understanding between an organization and its public'.

Because your organization is comparatively small it will be more advantageous if one of you is responsible for PR (which includes dealing with the press) and general publicity under the all embracing title of PRO. Your PRO should be out-going with his heart and soul in your project; his enthusiasm should be unmistakeable and infectious (voice and warmth of manner matter especially over the phone) and be able to:

(a) listen sympathetically and understandingly;
(b) cope with difficult situations without putting backs up, yet give as good as he gets when the occasion demands;
(c) put himself out for the good of the project or organization;
(d) take infinite care and trouble;
(e) put your organization's case convincingly and to the best advantage;
(f) get the best out of people;
(g) plan, see what needs doing and do it; be always on the ball and not let slip a single opportunity;
(h) co-operate completely with the Concert Manager;
(i) type if possible, even if only with two fingers;
(j) drive and have constant use of a car;
(k) be on the telephone.

He must also be physically fit and able to give a great deal of time and energy and be available during weekdays and at critical times. If a possible candidate has most or all of the other qualifications *but not the time*, look elsewhere. A PRO who is only available at weekends or evenings is a dead loss. Being a PRO is a time consuming business. You are, so to speak, always on duty. Make sure that whoever you approach to take on this job is fully aware of this.

A concert-promoting organization will need to have relationships with some or all of the following publics or groups according to the type of project:

(a) music lovers generally;
(b) established club members;
(c) potential members;
(d) the uninitiated you hope to win over;
(f) local authorities;
(g) education authorities;
(h) the various media;
(i) sponsors, prospective sponsors, guarantors and donors;
(j) clergy and parish councillors;
(k) venue managements;
(l) local music teachers and schools;
(m) the general community.

The art, and it is an art, of the practice of PR is the putting across of what

14

your organization is doing, working for and why, in such a way as to give it an image which will engender an appreciative understanding by all its publics that will lead to financial and other forms of help, build up goodwill, generate an enthusiasm that will swell the ranks of supporters, and sell your promotions.

PR has a general side which is very much the responsibility of the whole committee. This is not realised nearly enough, yet is tremendously important for the success of your project. The general side of PR covers: backing up the PRO; assisting with certain forms of publicity; and fieldwork.

Backing up your PRO. Once he or she has made contacts, spread information about your organization, worked to gain goodwill and good working relationships it may then be the turn of the committee members to carry on— the treasurer to work out details with sponsors or guarantors; the Concert Manager to cope with venue staff and so on.

Assisting with publicity. As many of the committee as possible will be needed to help distribute posters, leaflets and brochures. Your organization will need all the goodwill possible. They must, therefore, show it up in as favourable a light as possible. They must put themselves in the place of those they will be approaching: they must approach prospective site owners at slack times when, with luck, they will put a poster up at once; they must ask permission to put up posters or leave leaflets and brochures; they must try to see someone in authority and gain their interest and support; and they must go armed with drawing pins or sellotape. This can ensure that a poster or leaflet goes up at once.

Fieldwork. PR fieldwork consists of using the personal approach to enhance your organization's image and build audiences or club membership and is all done by talking to anyone and everyone wherever you happen to be. When you've done it the first time, talking to strangers is easy and becomes easier all the time. People don't mind and are often grateful especially the lonely ones.

General Publicity. Having planned the programme content, prices and subscription rates and other lures of a season, a festival or a single concert to appeal to as wide a field of music-lovers as possible, you must spread the good news throughout that field, including that of the advantages of membership where clubs are concerned.

Use every feasible method of publicity coupled with PR that you can or you will court failure. One method of publicity is not enough. Nor are two or more. You cannot hope to fill auditoriums or subscription and membership lists unless you reach out in as many different ways as possible.

15

Posters and leaflets. Both are essential, but give thought to the size of the posters. The big ones are expensive to produce and difficult to place unless you can afford to rent display sites. Few people have room for them. Far more practical is the A4 size for which there is little difficulty in finding homes. But whatever their size, posters and leaflets must be striking in design and layout so that the important parts leap to the eye (see Appendices 7, 8, 9 & 10).

Where to display posters and leaflets. You are trying to catch people in all walks of life and may catch a music-lover anywhere. So, do not concentrate on music, record or musical instrument shops. Posters and leaflets should be on view everywhere: bookshops, sub-post offices, hairdressers, food shops, travel agents, building societies, waiting rooms, staff notice boards in offices, hospitals, banks, local authority buildings, further education buildings, information bureaux, schools, church halls, concert venues, libraries and so on. In fact, use your library to spread the news. Vans are constantly running between libraries. Take your publicity to your library and ask if it can be distributed for display at others. It will then be sent to the central library of your area and sent out from there, usually being put on show about a fortnight before your event. Always attach a note of thanks to the Chief Librarian of the central library together with your address and a list of the libraries where you would like your publicity displayed.

You should also try to have publicity on show at other club or society meetings such as those of the WI, handicraft, debating, history, choral, orchestral societies and so on. Offer to give a reciprocal service. Publicity should also be displayed in your homes.

It does not pay to do an indiscriminate door to door leaflet drop. Far better to leave small piles for take-away in libraries and other strategic spots. Or, punch holes in the top left hand corners and string several together to hang in shops, waiting rooms etc., so saving them from being hidden under magazines or goods. Always have leaflets with you. Club's seasonal festival brochures must also be displayed as widely as possible as well as carried for fieldwork.

Paid display advertising in the press etc. This is expensive and there are other ways of getting news of your project into the papers. On the other hand such an advertisement will carry all the information that you want, whereas a press review or diary entry may not, indeed may not even be printed.

Free publicity in the press and other publications. Most local papers carry 'what's on' diaries as do some magazines. Entry is free but what goes in is at the compiler's discretion. Such diaries are also carried by county magazines, RAA and SAC publications, local authority leisure diaries, tourist board diaries, some parish magazines and so on. Your area tourist board will supply you on request with special forms to complete with event information. Most local papers are glad to include previews of your events or features about your organization especially if you can supply photos. However, editors never guarantee to put previews in exactly when you want them in, or even at all. Keep copy short: main points about artists, the programme, venue, date, time, a brief note about your organization, and a name and phone number for people to contact for enquiries.

Take previews to all your local papers. It is thought that this will not work but in practice I have found that it does. It may need a personal contact every time but I can usually count on something even if only a paragraph in each. So much depends on making yourself personally known to the editors or reporters and gaining their interest and sympathetic support. If, in spite of taking copy in well in advance and talking to the right people, nothing appears, and if this happens repeatedly, go to the top and put your case clearly and firmly to the chief editor. This does work.

Reviews of events are also a form of publicity in that they keep your organization in the public eye. Some papers send competent critics. Others may ask you to find one. But whoever does write the review must be given a couple of complimentary tickets: never one only. County magazines, RAA news sheets and publications may also fit in short editorials from time to time and use photos. Monthly and quarterly publications need copy a long way in advance. If your county magazine does not cover musical events try to change the editor's mind. Offer to write the copy. You might even find yourself appointed as editor of a Musical Corner. You may also achieve free publicity in the form of a published letter to the editor of a paper or magazine in which you put over a point of view about your organization or project.

Exhibitions. Shops, libraries, building societies, art centres etc. may be happy for you to stage exhibitions in their windows or buildings: these could include notices about dates, venues, prices, club information, festival information and photos of the artists, the venue or your club in action. Exhibitions must be striking and tasteful. Tattiness will only lead to expectations of tatty concert presentations and harm your image.

Radio and TV publicity may be had through: (a) local BBC or independent radio stations. No guarantees are made but they will do their best to mention your events and may even arrange interviews with artists or for you to talk about your event (see Appendix 3); (b) a live broadcast or a recording for later broadcasting of a concert. Though not so certain this is valuable publicity if it does come off. It is a matter of coming up with a programme that attracts the BBC enough to want to use it. Submit your programmes, as soon as they are settled, to the music section of the BBC in London or in your region, from where it will be channelled to the appropriate producers who will contact you if they are interested. If so, keep your fingers crossed that the venue's acoustics are suitable. An engineer will be sent to find out and if they aren't that will be that. But you will never know if you don't try and if it does come off it will give your project a tremendous boost, though the fee paid is not large; (c) there is always the chance that BBC TV or ITV might be interested in televising part of your festival or concert (see also Appendix 3).

Car stickers ensure that your project is made known where other types of publicity may not reach; and the *sale of pencils, beer mats, tee-shirts etc, emblazoned with your organization's logo and name*, are also used. The initial expense is costly however.

Last but very much not least *word of mouth* is one of the most important methods of publicity. There can never be enough of it. All successful clubs and promoters stress this as vehemently as I do. Impress the importance of word of mouth on everyone—committee, club members, helpers and friends. It is the personal approach at work again, and where local events are concerned you cannot do without it.

6. PLANNING

PROGRAMME CONTENT—MUSIC AND ARTISTS

A practical approach to your choice of music and artists is essential. Your aim must be to promote the best music performed in the best possible way by the right artists, but it is the planning of this that will count for so much. Plan badly and you put people off. Plan well and you attract good audiences or large memberships. And plan well you must if you are to survive, which means that when planning for local musical events programmes and artists should be chosen to appeal to as wide a field of music-lovers as possible. You cannot afford to be too specialised or avant-garde or to promote whole programmes of little or unknown works, contemporary or new works. People shy away from the unknown. There are not enough local people with such tastes to make it a viable proposition to cater exclusively for them, even with guarantees against loss. In a club's season of concerts you might get away with one such concert but no more, and, if you must have one, sandwich it between two popular ones and *not* at the beginning when your aim must be to attract everyone that you can.

The greater part of any local audience or club membership consists of people wanting to hear familiar, well-loved works, or unfamiliar works by composers they do know. However, this does not mean that programme content should be limited entirely to such works. Far from it, or the rare, the not-so-well-known, the contemporary and the new will never be heard. Nor will NFMS guarantees or WRAA/RAA/SAC grant aid or guarantees amount to much, if anything, if such works are not included (see Appendix 2). By including such works you will reap a bonus—the adding to your audience of the specialists who might not otherwise have come. Building up your audience should be part of your programme selection policy, for it can make the difference between success and failure and must never be ignored. Music, the form it takes (recitals, chamber music, orchestral, voice, choral, strings, piano, wind etc.) and the artists must be chosen to reach, attract, edify, give pleasure to and draw the greatest number of all ages of all types of music-lovers as possible.

Different types and forms of music attract different audiences. Just as a wily angler uses various lures to attract, hook and bring different species of fish to the net, so a wily programme selector should use varying lures to bring as many people into each concert as possible. A piano recital which attracts lovers of piano music also draws those who come for the music regardless of the instrument. If the pianist is well-known even more will come. If it is a popular programme still more will be attracted. If one of the works is new or different in some way it will pick up a few specialists, and every ticket sold counts. Similarly a piano ensemble is likely to attract a larger audience than an all wind or string ensemble, and if a voice is added you will draw in those who enjoy singing. Song recitals are not popular on the whole unless given by celebrated artists (whom you probably can't afford) but put a singer with, say, clarinet, piano or violin and a piano or with more than one singer and a much larger audience will turn up. Popular programmes will draw good audiences even if the artists are not so well known. Try where practicable, to include 'O' and 'A' level set works. As any one of your concerts (clubs especially) could be the first for those feeling their way, it behoves you to plan programmes that will ensure it will not also be their last!

Artists must also be chosen with care. The greater their name the greater their pulling power. Fees will be high but the extra expense is justified provided the seating capacity makes it a viable proposition or you can get sponsorship. But do not forget the outstanding young artists. Just as you can get away with slipping unfamiliar works between the familiar, so you can do the same with lesser-known names between the greater. Indeed, you should use the greater to subsidise the lesser.

Be discerning and discriminating in the planning of programme content both with the music and the artists. Considerable skill is needed to balance the music content both in one concert and a series of concerts and should be left to the experts—your music advisers or, if you are in doubt, seek outside advice. RAAs have music officers especially to advise on this, and artists' agents may also advise and, on request, plan an entire concert series or festival to suit your requirements and budget.

Agreeing the programmes of concerts may take time for, though you may know what you want, the artists may not always be able to oblige. They may not have the requested works in their repertoires, in which case, unless they can be sure of performing them again, it may not be worth their while learning them. They may have the requested works in their repertoire but due to heavy commitments not have enough time to work them up to concert pitch. Most will do their best to oblige but yours will not be the only organization requesting particular works, and they must draw the line somewhere. So, the sooner your request goes in the better, though even then you must still be prepared to accept a programme mainly of the artist's choice. The celebrated impresario, Wilfrid Van Wyck has strong feelings on programme choice: 'In the long run, it is far better to leave the choice of works to the artists. They know their capabilities, where they excel, the works that suit them or that they suit. There is no harm in putting forward suggestions and your reasons for them, but, if an artist feels that he really cannot do them justice then don't press the matter but abide by their ideas or choose an artist suited to the works you would like. Be discerning where young artists are concerned. Don't ask for great and demanding works, for this harms rather than helps, as they may feel that they should oblige for fear of losing the booking and will attempt to do their best. But it will not be the best that will come after years of experience mastering their technique and maturing and you will be landed with an unfinished, uninspiring and uninspired performance that will send people away thinking that the artist isn't much good when, in fact, he or she is outstanding in the works that he or she is capable of performing at that stage in his or her career. Furthermore it is enough to put people off the works that these youngsters have felt obliged to play against their better judgement.'

On the other hand, there are young artists who offer works far beyond them. I once heard a young pianist thunder through Beethoven's Hammerklavier Sonata with a deadly sameness that had his audience (a private club in a drawing room) fidgeting, bored and longing for the end before he was a quarter of the way through. He did himself great harm that night.

Seek artists who, at whatever stage in their careers they may be, can give a special quality to a performance, be it a familiar work or one you thought you might not like. Be extremely discriminating in your choice of artists. Always see and hear the lesser or unknown ones before engaging them. If they leave you totally unmoved, pass them by. Aim to promote concerts which as well as being enjoyable, broaden musical horizons, edify, stimulate interest, curiosity and the greater appreciation of music performed by fine but the right artists for the works, according to whatever stage of their careers they have reached at the time. However well-known or unknown the artists or the music, once you have established the reputation for all your concerts being first-rate in every respect you will increase your audiences and your membership, for you will have won your public's trust.

PROGRAMME BROCHURES, PROGRAMME NOTES

Strictly speaking, a programme is simply a list of the successive items of any entertainment or of a series of entertainments and their successive items and the artists taking part. Add anything else such as notes on each item and each artist, information about the promoting organization etc., and technically it them becomes a programme-brochure.

Programme brochures must be made to work for you: to give information, to enhance your organization's image and build up goodwill; and to sell your organization and its concerts. Though inanimate they are vital links between your organization and its public and must be designed to do a great deal of PR work. Therefore, both informatively and aesthetically it is imperative that they should impress enough for people to want to show them to others and pass them on. They must be striking enough to attract attention, yet tasteful in colour, lettering and lay-out. People are far more likely to join or support a prosperous rather than an impoverished organization so that, even if working on a shoestring, you must appear to be prosperous. And one way of doing this is by having brochures that look as good and as professional as possible, but the costs of which can be partly or completely offset by the sale of advertising space and their own sale.

Clubs' Season's Brochures and Festival Brochures. The form and size will depend on the amount of information that you can afford to include. They may be small booklets (Luton Music Club uses this type as they promote 26 concerts at weekly intervals during a season), larger booklets, often used for music festivals or folders of thin card or good quality paper. I do not recommend the use of several sheets of paper clipped together, or single sheets. They will do absolutely nothing for your image, are unwieldy, soon become scruffy and people will not be so likely to carry them around and show to others as they would neat booklets or folders. Be practical over the size, shape and weight of brochures. It is no use choosing a certain shape or size only to find, when printed, that it doesn't fit the envelopes. The total weight of a brochure, possible covering letters, enrolment form (if separate from brochure) and other literature plus the envelope should be planned not to exceed the minimum postal rate.

A Club's Season's brochure should contain everything possible to lure and hook old and new members and boost the sale of non-member tickets (see Appendix 8). A Festival Programme-Brochure is normally designed to carry full information about each concert so that it can also be used as a programme at each concert, thereby saving considerable expense (see Appendix 9). The more information that can be packed into seasonal and festival brochures the better they will serve you.

Concert programme-brochures may be in booklet form, the pages being stapled into a cover of coloured card or good quality paper; or in booklet form without a separate cover, the outer pages being treated as a cover. Again, I do not recommend sheets of paper clipped together or single sheets, they look amateurish, and will do nothing to help your image. For a Trial Concert leading, you hope, to the founding of a club, or for a new club's Inaugural Concert the programme cover should be designed accordingly to suit the occasion. Single Concert programme covers should be designed to suit the occasion (see illustration page 23, and Appendix 10).

PROGRAMME NOTES

Programme notes should be understandable to everyone, not just to the musically erudite, neither too technical nor yet talking down but guiding audiences through the music, showing what the composer is trying to do and setting the musical scene. These notes should be written by musicians or music teachers familiar with, or who will familiarize themselves with, the music and performances of the works before writing them. Trouble should be taken to obtain scores, music or records by borrowing from libraries, friends or acquaintances where necessary. Where works are unknown, new, or it is impossible to obtain scores, it may be possible for the composer or artists to supply notes, or notes can be obtained from artists' agents or music publishers, but in that case there may be a copyright fee to pay. It is important to head the notes of each work with its movements or parts where there are any. Apart from indicating the mood this is also a guide to the less knowledgeable as to when and when not to applaud. It is most important that the notes on the works being played should be so arranged that a page does *not* have to be turned over during a movement, section, part or piece: nothing is worse than hearing the turning of hundreds of pages during the music.

PRINTING AND DUPLICATING

The reproduction of programmes, brochures, posters, leaflets and so on should be of as high a quality as possible for the price you can afford. There are various methods of printing and duplicating, which includes photocopying, and often a combination of these methods may be used to produce the best effects at the most reasonable cost. The Yellow Pages list numerous printing and duplicating firms and those using combined methods. Your best policy is

Woking Music Club
1979–1980
GRAND OPENING CONCERT
Sponsored by B·A·T (U.K. and Export) Ltd

Tuesday, 16th October
at 8.15 pm
Woking Centre Halls

London Mozart Players

Conductor: *Harry Blech*
Solo Violin: *Maureen Smith*

Programme 20p.   56th Season

Programme design for a sponsored concert.

to consult various firms to discover which can satisfy your needs as economically as possible. The cost of duplicating can be reduced by cutting your own stencils, doing your own duplicating and your own artwork.

Artwork is the creation in black and white of anything which cannot be printed by normal type-setting methods, so that it can be photographed and made into a block or plate. It may include the use of Letraset or something similar, hand lettering, designs, drawings or the pasting on of black and white cut-out pictures, logos etc.

The printer will advise you as to how much can be fitted into a page or a leaflet. Ideally copy should be typed with double spacing between lines to allow room for printers' remarks, corrections or alterations. For this 'job-printing', you will probably see proofs at two stages. First, galley or 'slip' proofs on which you make clear corrections and alterations, which should be kept to a minimum or you may be charged extra except for printers' errors. Secondly, page proofs: the corrected galleys made into pages with page numbers, headlines, space for photos etc. At this stage, printers' errors excepted, it is extremely expensive to make corrections, additions or withdrawals.

NOTE Not all printing firms may accept artwork if its creator is not a chapel member of a union.

PIANOS: HIRING, BUYING, CARE AND GENERAL INFORMATION

Although one of the amateur promoter's biggest headaches, the provision of a suitable piano, if and when needed, is of the utmost importance because:

1. Artists cannot do justice to the music or themselves without the right tools and, unlike other instrumentalists, pianists cannot take their instruments with them. Some pianists will only consent to give recitals on full-sized concert grands and may even request certain makes and numbers, only accepting engagements on the understanding that such a piano is provided, this being written into their contract.
2. Ensembles need to be properly balanced so that, for instance, what is right for a recital might be too big (in sound) for a piano or string ensemble.
3. Lovers of piano works can be extremely fussy about pianos and many will not attend concerts unless a first-rate instrument is provided.
4. In order to thrive, your organization must earn a reputation for promoting high standard concerts which must include the provision of first-rate pianos when needed.
5. You have an obligation—music clubs especially—to present music at its best, which must include the use of the best possible piano.

Few venues boast a first-rate, full-sized concert grand though many may have smaller models which, if of good quality and in good condition, may just suffice for most piano, string, wind or voice ensembles, though some may need at least a 'B' sized one for particular works. But, for a full blooded piano recital nothing less than a top quality, full-sized concert grand should be provided. You might just get away with a 'B' size but this must be discussed with the pianist.

If you do not have the right piano for the job in situ then you should hire, borrow or, ideally, if promoting regularly, buy one.

Hiring a piano. The cost varies from firm to firm but is chiefly governed by the distance the piano must travel. Sunday deliveries and collections cost more than weekday ones. Many reputable firms include the cost of tuning in the hire price and provide their own tuners.

Assistance with cost of hiring: Grant Aid. In England and Wales, subject to certain conditions and the discretion of music advisory panels of your RAA/WRAA you may be eligible for Direct Aid. In Scotland organizations applying to the SAC for financial assistance in respect of public performances should include the cost of piano hire in their applications. This item of expenditure will then be taken into account when the Council decides on the amount of its offer (see Appendix 2). *Sponsorship and donations* should also be sought. *Insurance.* It is essential to insure a hired piano, it being your risk once the piano is out of the hands of the removers until they again take charge of it. Hire firms advise on the conditions of insurance. NFMS affiliated clubs can benefit from the advantageous terms which the NFMS secures for its members. Otherwise, shop around.

Where to find a piano.

(a) The Yellow Pages list firms hiring out pianos.
(b) *The Concert Piano in Scotland,* a report to the SAC 1972 (available from SAC, 19 Charlotte Sq. Edinburgh, EHD2 4DF) includes a catalogue of concert pianos in Scotland, states their situation, make, size, owners, including piano-hire firms, and availability for hire.
(c) Some RAAs in England own 'public pianos' for hire including the Yorkshire RAA, Lincoln & Humberside Arts, South West Arts and North West Arts.
(d) In Wales there are several travelling (peripatetic) pianos for hire and several strategically placed pianos for hire in situ (enquiries to WRAAs or the WAC).
(e) Some music clubs own pianos which may be hired (enquiries to the NFMS/RAAs/WRAAs/SAC).
(f) In Northern Ireland pianos can be hired from Messrs Tughan-Crane, 45 Fountain St., Belfast 1.

Booking a piano. The sooner you do this, even 18 months ahead, the greater your chance of getting one when you want it, otherwise you may have to fit the concert to when a piano is available.

Borrowing a piano. If someone is willing to lend a first-rate grand, it may well pay to borrow it, provided that you can find a firm experienced in moving or willing to be trained to move a grand piano; also a tuner-technician experienced in regulating and tuning grands to concert pitch. A borrowed piano must be insured while out of its owners' hands.

Buying a piano is the ideal solution and not impossible for clubs in spite of high prices. Nor need it be new if expertly reconditioned. Some firms will actually supply a piano before it is paid for, in order to help you raise part of the cost with recitals on it by celebrated pianists happy to assist. This has been done most successfully by Bedford Music Club.

The NFMS administers a fund created in 1955 by the Arts Council, from which any affiliated chamber music society in England may obtain a loan on easy terms for the purchasing or reconditioning of a pianoforte. Many clubs have been enabled to buy their pianos through this scheme. In this event there is a stipulation that the piano shall be made available for other affiliated clubs to hire. In Wales a certain amount of financial help, on the same terms (that the piano must be available for hire to other promoters), may in some cases be had by concert-promoting bodies from the WRAAs. In Scotland financial assistance may be offered by the SAC to music clubs towards the purchase or improvement of pianos. Contact the Music Department of the SAC for terms and conditions. Sponsorship and donations should also be sought and funds raised by special events. The more your self-help the greater your chance of official help.

When buying a piano great care should be taken in selecting a suitable instrument to satisfy all criteria involved, including size and seating capacity of the hall and the reasonable wishes of musicians likely to play on it. Help in this matter can be sought from the Piano Advisory Service who are able to provide impartial advice and assessment need. (Enquiries to: The Director & Administrator, Piano Advisory Service, The Cloisters, 11 Salem Rd., London W2 4BU. Tel: 01 221 0990/10).

Care of pianos. The importance of first-class maintainence cannot be overstressed. Concert pianos are valuable assets and it is simply throwing money away to put out a large lump sum as the initial purchase price and then proceed to ruin the instrument through ignorance and neglect. It should be the aim of every concert-promoting organization to ask for and be prepared to pay for the very best servicing of their instruments.

Care, storage and removal of pianos (See Appendix 13).

Delivery of hired piano. The Concert Manager or deputy should be present when a hired piano is delivered to ensure its correct placing. If an artist subsequently wants its position altered take great care.

Overcoming platform problems. Many modern platforms are made of chipboard, which does not always stand up to half a ton of piano, tremendous weight being concentrated under each wheel as under a stilletto heel. Indeed serious damage has been done to grands when legs have broken through such staging. However, the danger can be removed by spreading the weight by placing a two foot square of thick sheet steel (as at Farnham Maltings) or a two foot square of $\frac{3}{4}''$ wood (as at Woking) under each wheel.

7. THE LAW, OFFICIAL RULES & PITFALLS

MUSIC, SINGING AND DANCING LICENCE

Throughout the country there are areas where it is obligatory to obtain a *Music, Singing and Dancing Licence* for the premises in which it is intended to promote public entertainments of that nature including concerts whether or not an admittance charge is made. *NOTE* It is the venue that is licenced: not the promoter.

There are two types of licence. (a) The *Annual MS&D Licence* granted for premises such as concert, civic, village, school halls, leisure centres etc., which are used regularly for such entertainments, and (b) the *Occasional MS&D Licence* granted occasionally for premises used for such public entertainments such as churches, school, institute, village, or church halls etc. These licences are granted subject to compliance with the Regulations and Conditions 'for the time being in force made by the Licensing Authority', in most cases, County or borough councils. The regulations and conditions vary from area to area and authority to authority but will all have the same interest at heart—public safety.

Information on whether a licence is required and the regulations can be obtained in most cases either from the Public Control Department of your county council; or from the Housing and Environmental Health or Building Department of your borough council. Or, you may make preliminary enquiries of the Fire Service. You will find everyone most helpful and happy to advise on how you can most easily and economically adapt premises to comply with the regulations governing the issue of an Occasional Licence.

In the case of Annual Licences, regulations must be observed to the letter, whereas there is some leeway with Occasional Licences. The cost of either type of licence is minimal, the Occasional being less than the Annual, and varies from area to area.

The authorities will, of course, need to see the premises and know exactly what is intended therein and will want to ensure that you have complied with their advice in adapting them to meet the regulations. Should you be found flagrantly ignoring this, or should you risk putting on a concert in unlicenced premises and this is discovered, then, although the Licencing Authority has no power to prevent or stop the concert, you are liable to be fined. Furthermore, in such circumstances should there be a fire or an accident caused by your failing to comply which leads to claims on your insurance there is every possibility that the insurance company would refuse to recognise the claims.

With regard to private clubs it would seem that no licence is required for the concert venue provided that admission to the concerts is by subscription and guests paid for by those inviting them. Nevertheless, private clubs and promoters in areas where licences are not required would do well, for their own peace of mind, to seek advice from the Fire Service on precautions which, though not enforceable, it would be wise to take for the enhancement of their audiences' safety.

PERFORMING RIGHT

No musical work within copyright may be performed in public except under certain conditions (See Appendix 11 and NFMS Performing Right Scheme below.) Therefore, if you are using a venue not holding a Performing Right Society Licence, are not NFMS affiliated and wish to promote a public concert of such works, permission for their performance must be obtained from the Performing Right Society (PRS). There will also be a Performing Right fee to pay. Permission to perform works not under the control of the PRS must be obtained from the copyright holder(s), usually the publisher.

PRS/NFMS Agreement for Concerts promoted in Halls not holding a PRS Licence.
The NFMS has an agreement with the PRS concerning the payment of performing right fees by affiliated societies, on works in the PRS repertoire, which are performed in halls not holding a PRS licence. The NFMS pays a global sum annually to the PRS, and recoups this amount by charging a compulsory tariff to societies which promote concerts in unlicensed halls. This annual payment, which covers calendar years, completely absolves such affiliated societies from any other performing right payment for these performances. Payment is called for in January each year at the same time as the annual NFMS subscription is paid. The tariff is also payable in full by societies which promote concerts in both licensed and unlicensed halls. Only those societies which, in a year, never promote a concert in an unlicensed hall are exempted from payment of the tariff. *Concerts Promoted in Halls holding a PRS Licence.* When a concert is promoted in a hall holding a PRS licence, the hall manager can make a charge to the promoting society to cover the performance of works in the PRS repertoire.

In order that the block sum paid by the NFMS may be equitably distributed to the copyright holders, every affiliated society must send a copy of its concert programme to the Music Classification Officer, Performing Right Society, 29/33 Berners St., London W1P 4AA. Programmes can be sent to the PRS in a batch at the end of each concert season. The PRS provides a franked addressed sticker for this purpose, one of which is sent each year to society secretaries with the Spring edition of the News Bulletin. If the return is made on an official form issued by proprietors of licensed halls, the promoter's name should be given and shown as an affiliated society of the NFMS. For recitals, the name of artists should be included. It will help the PRS if the details mentioned below are, where necessary added to the printed or duplicated programme.

1. Full titles of all works performed, including individual titles of songs and carols.
2. Particulars of:
(a) the arranger or editor and publisher of early works and the arranger of non-copyright works;
(c) the translator of a work sung in other than the original language;
(d) the type of accompaniment used.
3. Name, address and approximate capacity of the concert premises used.

THE TAPE RECORDING OF CONCERTS

If you wish to tape record your concerts, written permission must be sought and gained both from the artists and the ISM and there is no guarantee that it will be given. For, although in many cases there would be no question of such a tape being used commercially, there is always that risk. In *A Guide to the Essential Background to a Musical Career,* Ian Wallace says, 'Artists have no opportunity to approve the balance or quality of the recording nor the guarantee that some slight mishap in their performance will not be played over and over to friends with the preamble 'Here's where the famous so and so gets the words wrong'. Also it may well be that they don't want the added pressure of a recording being made of a live concert.'

It is an offence (punishable by fine and/or imprisonment) to make a record directly or indirectly from the performance of any musician without the consent in writing of the performers.

To help artists to deal with requests for permission to tape-record a concert, the ISM has firstly included a clause on this matter in the ISM Standard Artists' Contract (General Condition 6) and secondly has received the co-operation of the NFMS in advising Music Societies to approach artists and the ISM for approval in advance.

The recording ruling applies to *all* promoters including those of private concerts, choral and amateur orchestral concerts, and rehearsals where professional performers and conductors are engaged.

NOTE. Some musicians, especially orchestral players and singers, may be members of the Musicians' Union or of Equity, which have their own regulations concerning tape recordings which must also be carefully observed *including* when professional 'stiffeners' are used in amateur orchestras.

Apply for permission well in advance. Considerable time can elapse before the application has done the rounds of the various artists (who may not be readily available), the ISM, the Musicians' Union or Equity. Where the general public is concerned there is a total ban on the tape recording of concerts. All promoters should make sure that audiences are warned to this effect by the display of prominent notices at the venue and in programmes.

PUBLIC LIABILITY INSURANCE

Where the public promoting of concerts is concerned it is essential to take out a Public Liability Insurance, which, if you are providing refreshments, should cover food poisoning. NFMS affiliated clubs are able to take advantage of the block insurance arranged by this organization at beneficial terms for its members.

COPYRIGHT (See Appendix 11)

8. CONCERT ORGANIZATION

ENGAGEMENT OF ARTISTS

Allow plenty of time for this, especially if your hearts are set on particular artists of some standing, when a year is scarcely long enough. Eighteen months gives a much greater chance of settling things your way, though two or three years may be needed when booking really big names. Some music clubs consistently work at least two years ahead to ensure booking those they really want. But, apart from that, it may take a considerable time, months, in fact, to book artists, especially where several consecutive (festival) or a season's (music club) concerts are involved, before everything is confirmed and contracts exchanged and signed.

Artists may be entirely free-lance; free-lance but also on one or more agent's books; solely with one agent; or solely with one agent but with their name on another's books with an arrangement between both agents. For instance, one agent may deal entirely with opera engagements for singers and not have the contacts to obtain recital bookings and so has an arrangement with an agent who does.

Where and how to find out about artists
1. *The Professional Register of Artists* produced by the Incorporated Society of Musicians (ISM) lists professional soloists, accompanists, chamber music ensembles, duo ensembles and conductors who are members of the ISM, together with addresses, telephone numbers or those of their agents. The Register is sent free to all NFMS clubs, Arts Associations and promoters of public concerts or is obtainable for a small sum from the Secretary of the ISM, 10 Stratford Place, London W1N 9AE.

2. *The British Music Year Book* lists:
(a) professional soloists, ensembles, conductors and composers, their phone numbers or those of their agents;
(b) artists' agents, their addresses and phone numbers;
(c) orchestras, major choirs, their addresses or their agents';
(d) colleges and schools of music who will supply information about students training as performers or emergent professional performers in need of the experience of public performances, albeit sometimes with private clubs;
(e) special music schools whose pupils might require public performances.

3. *Agents* supply on request and thence annually lists of their artists, their availability and fees (see Appendix 12).

4. *Regional Arts Associations* will advise about artists; some supply lists of artists or send information about outstanding performers. Some RAAs co-ordinate tours of artists. In Wales it is probable that this will be done via the WAMF. (See Appendix 2).

5. *The Scottish Arts Council (SAC)* supplies lists of performing musicians based in Scotland, but they are not exhaustive. The SAC also sends all Scottish promoters of public concerts lists of artists interested in making tours and then co-ordinates them. (See Appendix 2).

6. *Young Musicians' Liaison (YML)* acts as a link between all types of music club, including the smallest of private ones, and exceptionally outstanding young musicians at the start of their careers. On enquiry, YML recommends performers of recitals, oratorio, opera, chamber music or mixed concerts and establishes contact between societies and the artists of their choice. The service is free, the musicians receive their full fee and contribute towards postage and printing costs involved. Write to the founder, Colin D. Wainwright, Young Musicians Liaison, Lintalee, Austenwood Lane, Gerrards Cross, Bucks.

7. The music advisers on your committee, friends and aquaintances may know some artists personally.

8. Once it is known that you have formed a club or are promoting concerts you will be swamped with brochures, sometimes tapes or records from agents, artists, artists' personal representatives and so on.

9. Go to concerts including those promoted for young artists by the ISM, YML, SEAA, GLAA, NFMS, The Park Lane Group and so on, to see and hear for yourselves before deciding who to book.

31

10. Go to competitions (see Appendix 4 and *British Music Year Book*).

11. Listen to radio, watch TV and note artists of merit and interest.

First approach when engaging artists. If an artist is solely with one agent your first approach must be through that agent, otherwise you may deal directly with an artist. In the first instance phone the agent or artist rather than write; this is important in establishing a good working relationship as well as saving time. Your first approach must be in the nature of an enquiry as you will need to know the availability of an artist and his or her fee before you can go any further. There may be extras such as VAT, travelling expenses or a pianist's insistence on the use of a particular piano which may have to be hired and so on, all of which could upset your calculations and force a rethink.

If dealing through an agent and the artist is available but the fee unacceptable you can ask if this might be subject to negotiation. Until the matter is settled the next move is to ask the agent or artist to pencil in the engagement, you doing likewise. Pencilling is, literally, the pencilling of possible engagements into the diaries of the artist or agent and of the promoter until such time as they are confirmed or not. This does not commit you to that engagement. When juggling with a season's concerts you may find that you need to ask for alternative dates to be pencilled for particular artists. Confirmation should, nevertheless, be made as soon as possible. If you do keep an artist hanging on too long and they are offered a firm booking on the day of your proposed one you may, understandably, find that you will have to relinquish him or her if you cannot confirm within a stipulated time. The same can happen in reverse. When a booking is confirmed it is inked into everyone's diaries and any alternatives erased. You will then be asked or ask for a confirmation of the booking by letter.

Contracts should then be exchanged as a safeguard for yourselves, the agent (if concerned) and the artist. If agents are concerned they will send you a form in duplicate partly filled in and signed by themselves. You then complete the forms, sign them as confirmation and return *one* of them to the agent. The same contract will also have been sent to the artist for confirmation and signature. If dealing directly with an artist the ISM strongly recommend that the artist or promoter (you) use the ISM's *Standard Artists' Contract*. These are supplied in blocks of fifty by the ISM. Should you prefer not to use the ISM forms when dealing directly with an artist you should draw up something similar and use as above. *You cannot afford not to have a contract.*

Release from Contract may sometimes be sought by a young artist because a more prestigious booking than yours has been offered on the same day. What should you do? Unless there is a special clause allowing release in certain circumstances, there should be no question of releasing the artist no matter how important the proposed new engagement. However, if an artist says there is no question of his not honouring the contract, but is there any chance of altering his date with you because of an offer of a most important booking—what then? If the appeal is made far enough in advance and it is feasible to alter the date, I personally, would do all I could to arrange this and give him that big chance.

Cancellation due to illness or injury. No artists will willingly let you down (and even then it's not willingly) unless injury or illness makes it physically impossible for them to perform, or were they to do so it would lead to an inferior performance. Wind players and singers especially cannot perform properly when hampered by a cold, chest or throat infection which upsets breathing. Singers may suffer permanent damage to the vocal chords or be put out of action for a long time due to the enormous strain of trying to sing normally while their vocal chords are inflamed. So, if a singer cancels at short notice because of a cold, bear with him or her. What may seem trivial to you is very serious to them.

Replacement of artists who have to cancel. If they have been booked via an agent, the agent will inform you of the cancellation and is responsible for finding a deputy artist. If you have booked an artist directly, he or she will inform you of the cancellation and should find a deputy.

CARE OF ARTISTS

'M'mm . . . after such hospitality it should go well tonight,' John Lill, the celebrated pianist grinned as he wandered into my kitchen, set his empty tray on the table and rubbed his tummy appreciatively. And it did. Not for the food alone, though. Just as important, he'd been given the opportunity to disappear to a warm room with a bed where he could relax, gather himself and eat quietly on his own between rehearsal and concert. And that is what caring for artists means: looking after them in a way that will help them to give of their best.

Yet often, the well-being of artists is a matter of complete indifference to concert promoters. Artists are either plunged into social activities, driven to fend for themselves for fear of this, or completely ignored as in the following incredible, true story. A cellist and accompanist arrived at a venue for rehearsal. No one was there to welcome and show them round. They went in and rehearsed. No one appeared afterwards. Time passed. No one. They changed, looked into the hall and saw the audience settling in. Still no one to tell them when to begin. No refreshments. Nor did anyone appear at the end. All that duo ever saw of the promoters was a hand holding a cheque thrust round the dressing room door, and smartly withdrawn as the cheque was taken. And that was the only contact, if it could be called contact, from that music club!

A well-known accompanist says that so often promoters tend not to look on artists as ordinary human beings with the same needs of cloakroom facilities, the life-saving cup of tea after a long journey before getting down to rehearsing and so on. He also emphasises that it isn't just a question of providing a warm venue. There must also be warmth of welcome. Indifference to artists can, literally, make for indifferent performances, not done deliberately but as a natural outcome of the prevailing atmosphere. They also crave warmth, not just because they feel colder than usual but because they cannot give of their best if they are cold. Sluggish circulation leads to sluggish brain reaction with the consequent slowing of messages to muscles. And infinitesimal though that slowing may be it will be enough to take the edge off what would otherwise be a superb performance. Singers too must be warm and relaxed, for singing demands accurate working of the muscles controlling breathing (as does the playing of wind instruments). Singers also prefer the atmosphere not to be too dry.

Artists are, on the whole, very undemanding. They go out of their way not to be a bother, even to the extent of risking spoiling performances rather than upsetting their hosts.

Usually, all they ask for is somewhere to relax in warmth between rehearsal and concert, often a room on their own with a bed; remember too, that artists may have had a concert the day before yours or have spent the previous day recording, rehearsing or travelling a considerable distance to appear for you. They will also appreciate refreshments of some kind. Some eat well, others lightly, some not at all and some prefer to eat on their own. I have yet to meet an artist who will take alcohol before a concert, although I believe a few do. But after a concert is another matter when they often delight in relaxing with a drink.

What artists do not want before a concert is a social gathering to meet them, in the form of a drinks or dinner party.

Looking after artists takes common sense and an understanding personal approach right from the start. When booking artists let them or their agents know that you can offer hospitality between rehearsal and concert and overnight if necessary, and stress that they will be warm, able to relax and not be bothered. At this stage don't expect them to know when they will want to rehearse or want to stay overnight. They cannot plan in detail until they know their full season's commitments. Two or three weeks before the concert let them know when the venue will be available for rehearsal and ask what hospitality they will need. Take the precaution of asking if there is any food they cannot stand or that disagrees with them, and whether they prefer a light meal or whatever. Find out if they are coming by public transport or car.

If the latter send them a map clearly marking the venue and where they may park. If the former let them know the time of trains or buses and that you will meet them. All this means one less worry for them. Advise ladies of the dominant colours of the venue's decor.

The meal you offer between rehearsal and performance should be a moveable feast that can be produced quickly, won't spoil and if necessary can be taken to the venue. I find the ideal arrangement is a simple cold buffet, set out on the kitchen table. I ask my guests to help themselves to as much or as little as they wish. This meets with great approval, as they have a choice, don't feel they are being a nuisance and feel themselves at home in a friendly atmosphere. If a rehearsal is running late due to travel delays and so on, you may have to dash everything to the venue. When providing hospitality at a venue always take a sun-lounger, pillow, blanket, hot-water bottle, soap and towel. The delight shown at the trouble taken is most rewarding, and worrying in a way, because their surprise points to only one thing: that this rarely happens!

If you offer overnight hospitality it is helpful if pianists can be hosted where there is a piano. It needn't be special or a grand as long as there is something to play on. Never expect and certainly never ask an artist to perform for you in your home before a concert. If they want to they will, otherwise they will be conserving themselves for the rehearsal and concert. If hosting for the night after the concert you will find that most artists are pretty hungry and, now that they can relax, welcome a drink. For it is now that they need to unwind, sit back and enjoy themselves.

Most artists are glad of coffee, tea or soft drinks during the interval. Get it to them quickly and leave them. Few want to see anyone then and many ask to be guarded against this as people do sometimes try to slip in. Rehearsal refreshments may be required especially by orchestras and ensembles who often put in three hours. Hospitality for orchestras between rehearsal and concert must be at the venue because of shortage of time and lack of space at home. Obviously when catering for an orchestra a charge will have to be made. Often orchestra members or some of them will bring their own food and only need some form of drink. But do make sure that they are warm and as comfortable as possible with somewhere to relax. After the concert artists often appreciate a long, cool drink. See that this is waiting for them in the dressing room. Some artists may have a long journey and want to get off pretty smartly. It is a kindness to supply a packet of sandwiches and refill their thermos if they have one. Some clubs throw a party after a concert but this is by no means the rule or necessary.

When hosting artists you must plan to return them to the venue at the time *they* wish to be there. The ladies, especially, prefer to change at the venue to avoid spoiling long skirts. Time must also be allowed for warming up. You will be doing the artists a gross disservice if you do not plan accordingly: to keep artists on tenterhooks as to whether they will be late and not have time to change or warm up without a rush is asking for a bad start to a performance and may blight the whole concert. Also, a late start does not look well either for the artists or the promoter and must be avoided at all costs.

Just as an athlete warms up immediately before his race, so musicians, singers included, must warm up immediately before going on. It is important, therefore, if at all possible, to provide somewhere out of earshot for them to do this, even if it has to be the coffee bar. Towel and soap are most important at the venue. Most instrumentalists, especially string players, wash their hands before rehearsing, before the concert and during the interval to remove grease or sweat which can affect strings adversely or cause a finger to slip or stick on a note or string.

Be prepared to cope with any emergency: sewing buttons, pressing dresses, coping with coughs, headaches, tummy upsets. Artists who are well cared for look forward to appearing for you again, and word soon gets round that you are a good crowd to come to. Word also gets round if artists haven't been well cared for and they may never appear for you again or, given the choice of appearing for you or someone else, may well avoid you. Look after your artists and they will look after your concert. It is your job to get them onto the platform in the mood to give all they've got.

CONCERT MANAGEMENT

Concert management is a long-term operation stretched over many months which gradually gathers way, peaks with the concert and ends with the clearing up. Successful concert management is the result of good teamwork under the direction of a Concert Manager (CM) who, ideally, should have patience, common sense, stamina, ingenuity and diplomacy; be able to use the personal approach, plan, hold his or her own, and deal with emergencies; be tough, have the hide of an elephant and above all, foresight. A CM has the overall responsibility for everything remotely connected with mounting a concert or series of concerts. He or she must direct, correlate and channel everything into the main stream at the right moment; anticipate snags and avoid them; surmount problems; keep the hall management and staff happy and co-operative and the audience and artists happy; make sure the show goes on regardless as professionally as possible by keeping everything flowing and building to the successful climax.

It is a big and complicated job but gives enormous satisfaction. Because so much depends on it he or she should have a deputy assistant who knows what is happening, where all the information is kept, and is known enough at the venue to be able to carry on if necessary. A CM should be available during weekdays, weekends and the whole of the concert day or festival days. He or she should be on the phone, have a car and a great deal of time to give.

36

A CM must be able to call on other committee members to carry out certain tasks with the utmost reliability, especially the PRO or the whole thing will founder. They must all know their jobs and be prepared to pull their weight.

Concert management varies a certain amount according to the type of promotion—music club concert, festival, single concert; but, in general, concert management divides into three parts: pre-concert; day of concert; and post concert.

(A) PRE-CONCERT:

1. *Early matters.* Your budget has been worked out, venue selected, a satisfactory price agreed with the printer, and you have a rough idea of dates decided and the artists you hope to engage with alternatives chosen. The CM must then:

(a) book the venue, artists, piano or harpsichord (if required);

(b) prepare your brochure material by choosing and agreeing programmes with the artists (for early publicity and so that the writers of programme notes can set to work); and by obtaining artists' biographical notes and photos;

(c) arrange (if required) for the adaptation of the venue to comply with the regulations governing the granting of a *Music, Singing & Dancing Licence.*

Get your PRO to sell advertising space and get in the copy and artwork (set a deadline well in advance of when you really want it) and to fix deadlines with the printer for brochures and tickets. It is vital that tickets should be ready well before booking starts. Get him also to arrange for your ticket sales outlets; to book exhibition sites; to approach radio and TV organizations for publicity and coverage; and to find out copy dates for local press, monthlies, quarterlies and various diaries of events.

2. *Interim Matters.* Having set the wheels in motion you must now keep them turning as well as furthering the good work. Your PRO should:

(a) Chase up the artwork, programme notes, etc. Put them into copy form; discuss layout with printer; get everything to him on time.

(b) Plan the publicity campaign and run-up to your event. Organize a team for putting up posters and distributing leaflets. Give plenty of warning as to when this must start so that everyone will be free.

(c) Get publicity to monthlies, quarterlies etc. (it may be needed as much as three months in advance).

(d) Mount exhibitions about your event at intervals and at different sites throughout the interim period.

(e) Ensure, as the run-up period approaches (4–5 weeks before a concert or festival) that any printing so far not received is going according to plan so that everything will be to hand when you want it.

The CM should:
(a) Get patrons' or stewardship scheme under way 4–6 months before events;
(b) Mail and distribute advance news leaflets 4–6 months before events.
(c) Start the sale of festival programme brochures and advance booking at special rates (if any) 8–12 weeks ahead, or advance booking 4–8 weeks before concerts.
(d) Set in motion the planning of teams, each organized by one of the committee, to deal with:
(i) preparing venue: this may include putting out and possibly numbering seats, arranging floral decorations, sprucing the place up, checking dressing rooms and cloakrooms for toilet paper, soap, towels, cleanliness etc., and clearing up afterwards; (this also includes doing what is necessary to comply with the MS&D Licence if required);
(ii) refreshments if you have to do your own catering;
(iii) manning, as appropriate, the box-office before the festival or concerts and on concert nights, if this is not done for you;
(iv) front of house matters at concerts—manning the doors, programme selling, stewarding etc.

3. *Run-up to concert or festival* starting 4–5 weeks beforehand.
(a) During the first week the publicity team must get posters up, leaflets distributed and exhibitions mounted. The PRO must get previews, photos and diary information to the local press and, if your local authority includes your events in their advertising panels and leisure diary, check that their copy is correct and arrange for reviews to be made of concerts.
(b) Start normal ticket sales on agreed date.
(c) If getting radio or TV publicity or coverage, check final arrangements.
(d) About 14 days before the event, check when venue will be free for rehearsal, inform the artists, enquire if they need overnight hospitality etc. (see page 34).
(e) If hiring or borrowing a piano, check when it can be delivered at the venue; inform those concerned and arrange for tuning—normally after rehearsal. If you are responsible for the tuning of the piano, book a competent tuner-technician well in advance. If the piano is kept locked ensure the key is available for rehearsal, tuner and concert.
(f) About a week before the concert or festival, discuss final arrangements with the venue management for heating, lighting, seating, refreshments and bar, if done by them, or facilities for you to do same; use of dressing rooms and of somewhere for artists to warm up if the dressing rooms are unsuitable for this.
(g) Arrange for someone to turn the music for keyboard players if required. An unpopular but skilled and necessary job. Usually artists like to go

through the works with the turner before the concert. Ensure that the turner will be punctual.

(h) Order flowers and foliage for the platform etc. and a bouquet if you have a lady soloist with orchestra, or a suitable gift if a male.

(i) Send complimentary tickets to the press and, if required, the sponsors and officials of the NFMS/RAA/other clubs, and the artists themselves.

(j) Arrange for a Red Cross or St. John's Ambulance Brigade member to be present at the concert.

(k) Ensure that all operative committee members and teams know their posts for the event.

(l) Ask the treasurer to provide a float for programme sellers, also the box-office if operated by yourselves.

(m) Stand by for artists to contact you about the final arrangements—often not done until the day before the concert.

Throughout the run-up, the PRO and CM should spur on the committee and other helpers to increase their efforts in spreading the word and ticket selling, if this is not all done by the box-office.

(B) Day of concert or first and following days of festival

(a) *Morning:*

(i) If hiring a keyboard, see it in and positioned, or position resident piano if being used. Remove all finger marks and polish if necessary.

(ii) If putting out seating, check that your or the venue's team does this correctly and that seat numbering, if not permanent, is done the right way round.

(iii) If having to comply with regulations for a MS&D Licence, check that whatever must be done has been done.

(iv) Check dressing rooms and cloakrooms.

(v) Check that there are the correct number of chairs on the platform for the artists including one for the turner if required. Be prepared to provide other types of chairs if the venue's do not suit wind players or 'cellists.

(b) *Before Rehearsal*

(i) Meet artists at venue or station etc. Show them round the venue and offer refreshment.

(ii) Check platform lighting with artists and venue staff or your lighting expert.

(iii) See that artists have all they need including copies of the programme. They may ask you to stay awhile to see if they have got their balance right. Arrange a time to pick them up after rehearsal or to provide refreshment at the venue and then leave them to it.

(c) *After Rehearsal.* Take artists to where they are being hosted until the concert, or provide refreshments at the venue (see page 35). Impress on the hosts the importance of returning the artists to the venue when *they* want to be there.

(d) *Before the Concert*. CM and helpers should arrive half an hour before the doors open, which is usually half an hour before the concert starts.

(i) Check lighting again, including emergency exit lighting.

(ii) See artists to dressing rooms. Ensure they are not disturbed. Arrange for their interval refreshments. See that they have their complimentary tickets.

(iii) Keep an eye on the front of the house which should be running itself, that is the box-office, programme selling, stewarding etc.

(iv) Arrange for a 5 minute bell before the start of the concert and for latecomers to be kept out of the auditorium until a suitable moment to enter.

(v) Start concert punctually. Fetch artists from dressing rooms, open door to platform, start applause as artists walk through. Lighting to be dimmed at the same time.

(vi) Stand by to open and close platform door to let artists on and off between items.

(e) *During Interval*

(i) Lights up.

(ii) Check that artists have their refreshments and are *not* disturbed.

(iii) Make sure the interval bell is rung 5 minutes before start of second half.

(iv) Fetch artists to platform. Dim lights again.

(f) *After the Concert*

(i) Lights up.

(ii) Give artists a few moments before letting audience members into green room or to wherever they may meet them. Check that there are further refreshments for them.

(iii) Show audience members through if artists are happy to meet them.

(iv) If dealing directly with artists see that they have their cheques before leaving.

(v) Thank them and see them on their way or to their overnight hosts.

(vi) Make sure that those responsible have tidied the venue, replaced chairs if necessary, closed the piano and so on. Thank all helpers and venue staff.

(C) POST CONCERT

(i) Let the treasurer have the returns as soon as possible, i.e. number of seats taken, money taken for tickets, programmes and, if supplied by you, refreshments.

(ii) Look out for press reviews, keep copies and send others to the artists and sponsors where necessary.

(iii) Attend the post-mortem committee meeting, so that mistakes or slip-ups can be rectified for the next concert or festival.
(iv) Return all photos to agents or artists.

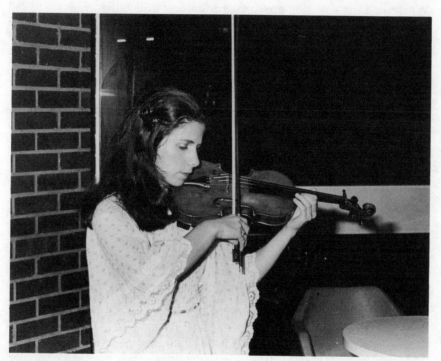

Maureen Smith "warming up" in a corner of the coffee bar before a concert.

SECTION II

Music Clubs

1. TYPES OF MUSIC CLUB

Whatever their size, non-profitmaking, concert-promoting music clubs fall into two main groups: those, most of whose concerts are open to the public as well as to members, in the future referred to as 'Open Clubs'; and those whose concerts are *only* open to members and invited guests, in future referred to as 'Private Clubs'.

1. *Open Clubs divide into:*
(a) those affiliated to the NFMS in England—by far the greater number;
(b) those affiliated to the NFMS in Scotland, who can take advantage of certain NFMS benefits but receive their guarantees from the SAC;
(c) those not affiliated to the NFMS in Scotland, who receive guarantees and aid from the SAC;
(d) those not affiliated to the NFMS in England and Wales, who may receive guarantees and/or grant aid from their RAAs/WRAAs as appropriate.

All open clubs are financed by means of all or some of the sources of income listed on page 6, and their organizations, concerts, fund-raising events etc. are advertised publicly. They serve the various publics of villages, towns, districts, schools (usually private or public schools), colleges, universities, hospitals, churches, banks, business houses and so on. They can be midday, lunchtime or summer music clubs, or the music side of Arts Societies which can affiliate if they wish to the NFMS. Abbotsholme Arts Society and the Royal Tunbridge Wells Green Room Society have such off-shoots. The number of concerts promoted during a season may vary from four to six or even more—Luton Music Club promotes twenty-six and the Manchester Midday Concerts' Society promotes weekly ones. All or most of the concerts arranged by NFMS affiliated clubs are given by professional musicians since financial assistance from official bodies is almost always only given for the professional element excluding any charity concerts (see Appendix 1). Non-affiliated clubs also promote mainly professional concerts, since the same conditions apply with regard to financial assistance.

Concert venues may be local authority halls, churches, school, university, college, hospital, parish, church halls, converted barns and so on. Members' Evenings or Events are also held by some open clubs. Of a more intimate nature they are usually held in smaller venues. Outings to other musical events are also organized. *NOTE*. These events must be open to the public if a club is a registered or recognized charity.

2. *Private Clubs*
(a) The small, drawing-room type whose concerts are held in private premises rather than hired venues.
(b) The larger club run by private or public schools, universities, colleges, hospitals, and other institutions, whose membership is made up of staff, pupils, parents, doctors, nurses, patients and friends as the case may be, and which has the advantage of captive audiences, larger numbers of invited guests and the use of their own halls and often a good piano.

Private Clubs are financed by subscriptions, charges for guests, donations and, where necessary, private fund-raising events. Because their concerts are not open to the public they are not eligible for affiliation with the NFMS and the consequent benefits, nor for assistance from RAAs/WRAAs/SAC. The smaller drawing room type clubs' concerts vary in number. Yet, though for obvious reasons there is not a lot to spend on artists, concerts of high standard can and should be achieved. The larger private clubs, especially those of schools, universities or colleges, are run more on the lines of open clubs for they are in the financial position of being able to engage professional performers at the going rates. Private clubs also run outings to other concerts, opera etc. and may, as open clubs do, have evenings when members perform for members. There is no public advertising of private clubs or their concerts.

2. THE ROLE OF MUSIC CLUBS IN THE MUSIC WORLD

Just how important and influential a role music clubs have come to play and must continue to play in the music world is not always realised. They do, in fact, occupy a unique place therein, with inter-related obligations and responsibilities both to their public, and to the music profession. For if they are to serve the former well they must also serve the latter equally well. On their committees' choice depends the quality of the performers, the music and its performance that they bring to their public; on them also to a very large extent depend the livelihoods of the professional musicians and the development of their careers. All clubs, whether NFMS affiliated or not, large, medium, small, private or school, are now so vital to the survival of the professional performance of chamber music or recitals that without them such performances in public would almost disappear. There just would not be enough work to go round or justify the artists' training in any number.

43

The aims of all clubs of whatever type should be based on those given in the NFMS draft for a 'model' Constitution for a Music Club: 'To promote, improve, develop and maintain public education in, and appreciation of, the art and science of music in all its aspects by the presentation of public concerts and recitals and in such other ways as the Club through its Committee, shall determine from time to time.' This will be achieved by:

1. Presenting concerts of only the best music performed by only the finest professionals at all stages in their careers, and the right ones for the works. (See *Programme Content* above and *The Music Club's Role in Relation to the Music Profession* below).

2. Understanding their role (according to type of club) in relation to the profession—artists, composers, conductors, teachers—and acting accordingly to ensure the continued fine performance, interpretation and composition of music.

3. Fostering future generations of music-lovers and concert-goers to carry on the good work and so preserve our musical heritage.

4. Bringing people to music and not just music to people.

5. Supporting amateur orchestral and choral societies who are also vital to the profession.

6. Helping to counteract the problem of general audience shortfall and so ensure the survival of our professional orchestras, conductors, and even perhaps our major concert halls, to say nothing of artists' agents and managements.

THE MUSIC CLUB'S ROLE IN RELATION TO THE MUSIC PROFESSION

(a) *Artists—the practical and constructive furthering of their careers by all clubs.*

I have used the adjectives 'practical', 'constructive' and 'all' with good reason. For, though it is an indisputable fact that all music clubs are indispensable to the building of artists' careers and that it is virtually impossible for them to advance without our concerts, it is also a fact that this is not widely realised, nor that we can do so much more for them by using a far more practical and constructive approach. But, in order to discover what each type of club can do and how the maximum help can be given, the practical approach is for us first to learn how an artist's career is built and the problems encountered on the way. For only then can we act constructively.

The 1978 report to the Gulbenkian Foundation on the Training of the Professional Musician states: 'If he or she is to stand a chance of becoming a professional violinist or pianist, the young musician should start to play seriously by the age of 7 or 8, and wind and brass players cannot normally leave it much later than about 11. . . . For the gifted young musician seeking professional training, important decisions have to be taken at about the age of 11. . . . By the age of 16, young instrumentalists should know the nature of their commitment to music. If they are talented this is generally the appropriate age for them to concentrate single-mindedly on preparing for a career in music.' In other words, they must begin to specialize long before other children are even giving thought to their futures.

Building a musician's career is an extremely lonely business which takes an enormous amount of self discipline and hard work. But hard work and the acquisition of superb technique and musicianship can only go so far in the making of a fine artist. There must also be the stimulation and experience of public performance and the acquisition of an attractive platform manner. So, exposure to audiences begins at a very early age at small concerts arranged by teachers. From seven onwards children are entered in competitive music festivals and perform in school concerts. Students at the special music schools will solo with the school orchestras or share recitals in public concerts. Some, as Menuhin School students do, appear in such concerts throughout the country and even abroad, though only the finest will be allowed to perform. Outstanding performers in ordinary schools will also need extra-mural appearances. Many take their turn as soloists with the county or national youth orchestras to which they belong and while at college or university will solo with college or university orchestras and give public recitals. During their final year, exceptional performers will be allowed to give extra-mural recitals and solo with amateur orchestras and choirs. Once graduated, would-be soloists must decide when to turn professional. Some may continue studying with the assistance of awards from the Gulbenkian Foundation, the Leverhulme, Martin or Countess of Munster Trusts etc. Others may want to begin their professional career at once. But whenever they do decide to launch out there are problems.

Professional promoters will not offer engagements without the production of favourable press reviews from national papers or proof of a successful broadcast. But the BBC, generally speaking, only offers auditions on the evidence that the intending soloist is already a professional musician—something of a vicious circle. The only way of breaking out of it seems to be by winning a competition or by a debut in a London public hall, it being virtually unknown for the national press to attend such an event elsewhere. Traditionally held at the Wigmore Hall, such debuts now also take place in the Purcell Room. In both cases would-be soloists or chamber music players can audition for sponsorship for such debuts to the Park Lane Group, the ISM, the NFMS, certain RAAs and other organizations which give financial help for such events. Few artists can afford to promote themselves.

Though the timing of debuts is vital, they cannot always be arranged to the artists' best advantage and they can only pray that the right moment has been chosen, that they will be in top form, that at least some of the press critics, agents, promoters etc., who have been invited will turn up and react favourably. But, even then, in most cases, agents do not manage young artists until they have established themselves, including competition winners. All that happens in most cases is that young artists, unless very lucky—for there is not even room for all the most outstanding with the exclusive agents—merely have their names added to an agent's list which is sent to promoters. There is no personal representation. If promoters want extra information they must apply for it. It is left to the young artists to send out their personal brochures or make personal contacts.

It is impossible for promoters to judge from brochures alone or recordings and this is a testing and heartbreaking time for young intending soloists or chamber music players. In the end it is only the most tenacious or the incredibly lucky who will survive and not necessarily the most outstanding or deserving. Nevertheless, many do well for the first year or two of their professional careers. Then, things begin to go wrong. Jobs fall frighteningly away, even for competition winners, except the one or two on exclusive agents' lists. Only the few, most distinguished soloists can live by solo work alone. The rest supplement their earnings by teaching and with ensemble work, but many of today's artists are being forced more and more to fall back almost entirely on this or even to turn completely to orchestral work. They seem to reach a dead end—the artists' and agents' nightmare—the black patch. How are they to advance without further regular public appearances, ideally eight or nine a month? Why aren't they getting them? I refer to the really outstanding young artists, competition winners and runners-up who began so well, who should have gone on rising but are not. As I see it there are several reasons.

1. Having done well for a year or two they quite rightly increase their fees, not a lot but enough to put them out of reach of the smaller music clubs whose existence depends on being able to engage low-fee artists. So one door is closed.

2. At the other end of the scale, they are not well enough known for the larger clubs to book them in quantity, for they depend on the big names to attract members (especially true of clubs in or near London or other major musical centres where they are competing against concerts of the highest order). So that door is only ajar.

3. On top of that there is the bottleneck created by there being too many would-be soloists on the market who somehow manage to secure bookings either by cut-price rates or by pricing themselves high and hoodwinking the less discriminating into believing that they are on a par with the really fine performers.

4. Where competition and award winners are concerned, the drop in bookings seems partly due to clubs feeling that they have done their duty by engaging them directly after their award, and partly to the misapprehen-

sion that having won an artist will always have work, so they needn't book them again.

5. The bottleneck is further jammed by the many young performers flooding this country from abroad, some of whom can't hold a candle to our own, and yet who will be preferred to British artists, on the false presumption that a foreign name guarantees an outstanding performer or that a foreign name has greater drawing power.

So how *do* artists break out of this black patch and back into the public eye to really establish themselves? They must again appear, as often as possible, in front of those that matter—agents, promoters, the press, conductors, BBC and recording company representatives, impresarios etc. But this can be difficult. For what is not generally known is that after the early sponsored debut recitals, unless a sponsor or patron can be found, artists must themselves finance their recitals at the South Bank, the Wigmore Hall, St. John's Smith Square etc. No one makes a profit, few break even, and most are considerably out of pocket. There are long waiting lists for these venues and only artists of some standing are considered for the more prestigious recitals. All of which inevitably leads to more falling by the wayside. But, I believe that much of the heartache and nightmare can be prevented if music clubs are more constructive in their approach to artists' careers and discriminating in those they engage and go on to support.

THE MUSIC CLUB'S ROLE IN FURTHERING ARTISTS' CAREERS

Concerts should be offered to really outstanding young musicians of all ages while they are still at school, including those at the special music schools, by:
(a) the small drawing-room-type private clubs;
(b) open clubs for members', or smaller events;
(c) school clubs for their most promising young musicians.

Even in these early days, such concerts begin to show up those cut out to be performers and give them a chance to build up confidence, learn to get the feel of an audience and how to project themselves.

Students still at college or university welcome extra-mural concerts with open arms but, unless high-flyers, they will not be allowed to perform outside their college until their final year and then only if outstanding. But this does mean that you can be sure of an excellent concert at very low rates set by the college, usually calculated to cover travelling expenses and a little pocket money. In the first instance you will have to take whoever is available but if you are particularly impressed with anyone you can request their appearance for another concert.

After graduating or finishing their post-graduate studies and training, young artists offer their services at low fees before making their London debuts or winning a competition or award, and at this stage they are still

47

entirely dependent on small private or open clubs and members' evenings of the larger clubs for recital or ensemble engagements and on amateur orchestral or choral societies for solo bookings. It is not economically viable, even with guarantees or grant aid, for large open or private clubs to use them in main concerts at this stage unless they have won a competition very early on. So, it is up to the smaller private, open, or larger clubs promoting members' events, to keep the most outstanding of these young artists employed.

During the early post-debut years or after winning a competition or award, fees are raised, often beyond the reach of small private or open clubs or what can be spent on larger clubs' members' evenings. These openings are still needed, however, for rehearsal concerts before big recitals and fees are often dropped for the sake of these concerts. Otherwise the newly-fledged professional moves up the music club ladder and it now becomes the turn of medium sized open or private clubs to provide the greater part of their recital or ensemble work, for, at this stage, only competition winners and the few lucky enough to earn phenomenally good debut reviews will make the large clubs as well. This is not to say that others are not so outstanding. Many are, and given the chance some at least could go to the top, and it is the small or medium sized clubs who can give them that chance. But providing engagements is only part of their responsibility: also it is their duty to invite programme selectors from large clubs, choral and orchestral societies to their young artists' concerts. They may be disappointed but, equally, if they are sufficiently impressed, though they may want to wait for greater maturity to develop before offering a booking, they will remember them and the next time the agents' lists come round a name will ring a bell and there may well be a job forthcoming.

This co-operative involvement between clubs in the furthering of artists' careers at all stages is most important and should be part of every club's policy. It begins with the smaller private clubs, school clubs or open clubs holding members' evenings offering hearings to outstanding performers still at school. Keep in touch while they are training and if their teacher considers them outstanding enough offer a concert in their final year. Find out if they are preparing for a London debut and offer a rehearsal concert for this vital event. Get the whole club interested and eager to help. Arrange a coach trip, if within reach; think of the tremendous fillip it will give them to know there are friends 'in front' to say nothing of the financial help it may provide. Work on the press to slip a piece in as a news item about your outing: it not only gets the artist's name around but helps to keep it in front of the public. If you have no sufficiently outstanding school leaver to help then concentrate on an outstanding college student. But remember that great discernment is needed in backing your hunch, but every now and again you will get your reward.

Members and committee members of the small private clubs should also

48

play their part in spreading the word about outstanding young artists. Interchange of news and information about artists should be part of any and every club's policy. The federal representatives and club delegates should also spread the word at NFMS national and regional meetings and conferences. But, important though all this is, in itself it does nothing to help the outstanding older young artists break out of that black patch in which, through no fault of their own, many find themselves after a flourishing start to their careers or after returning to the platform after lengthy sabbaticals for intensive study and repertoire building or periods abroad. It does nothing to widen the bottleneck caused by the larger clubs' dependence on engaging mainly well-known names in order to survive. Obviously, there must be a limit to the number of concerts that can be offered to rising artists, for these clubs must also keep the established artists going. After all, the rising artists will one day become established and still be in need of your concerts. I believe, however, that there should be a larger allocation than at present: in most cases at least two concerts per season for older young artists of outstanding merit.

Why not try obtaining sponsorship for such a concert? Explain to the prospective sponsor what these young people are up against and how important sponsors and clubs are in the furthering of their careers at their most critical stage and so in ensuring the preservation of our great musical heritage for posterity. This is possible and has been achieved at Woking where for three seasons they have now been able to include two such concerts, the first being sponsored by the Johnson Wax Arts Foundation and the second subsidised by the big names of the other concerts and NFMS/RAA financial aid.

Will people still want to join a club which only sports two or three big names in a season? I believe so, though it must be worked at in two ways: first, by making it seen that your club has the reputation for filling an important role in the music world by playing a vital part in advancing artists' careers; and secondly, by getting over to members, prospective members and the music loving public in general that when it comes down to it, it is they who do, quite literally, call the tune. Few people have the faintest idea of what goes into making an artist's career or a concert: that they are directly involved in helping artists establish themselves has never entered their heads.

What else can larger clubs do for the exceptionally outstanding young artists? A lot. Follow their careers. Adopt them as it were. One main concert is not enough. Offer another in a year or two. Try to get the BBC to record it. Offer them a rehearsal for an important recital as a main concert or members' evening, and put them in touch with other clubs who may be able to do likewise. Large clubs can be of immense help by offering their adopted young artist a concerto or vocal work with a professional chamber orchestra. Such a performance is priceless to them for it is almost impossible for a young artist yet not nationally known to obtain concerto or solo work with professional orchestras unless as a competition winner's prize. There is indeed much constructive help that can and should be given by all types of clubs by interchange of information and support between each other and the performing societies in their immediate locality and further afield. For instance in areas far from major musical centres, clubs could help one another and the artists by arranging tours: a tour might consist of a recital for one club, a solo with an orchestral or choral society ten miles away, another recital fifteen miles in another direction, a schools' concert somewhere else and so on. Travel expenses can be split among the promoters, cost of hotels is nullified by hosting the artists yourselves and fees are reduced according to the number of concerts. Artists and agents put in pleas for clubs to work out such tours.

Another way in which all clubs can help young artists is by letting them know how they 'come over' as regards dress, deportment, manner and performance. I am often asked for such appraisals because they really want to know so that they can rectify any faults. So, if asked for an honest opinion, take the askers at their word and give it constructively and diplomatically. It should also be remembered that our increased encouragement and help in furthering artists' careers will have considerable bearing on maintaining and enhancing this country's growing musical prestige abroad. For they can only become great with the help of regular public appearances and it is we, the music clubs, who can supply the bulk of them.

Composers' careers may be helped by commissioning a work, which is not as impossible as it may seem, for, subject to their approval, RAAs will provide the commission fee. Such commissions are extremely important as one composer, Michael Graubart, Principal of the Music Department, Morley College explains: 'The members come prepared to be in some way engaged in a relationship, not a take-it-or-leave-it commercial transaction. This means, too, that the composer himself can, in a pre-concert talk or social gathering or otherwise, demonstrate not just a few technical features of his piece in an informal way that is more effective than a learned programme note, but—much more importantly—can show the members that he is a human being just like them, with just the same problems of getting kids to school in the morning, working while the dog wants to go for a walk and so on; and that the reasons he writes such funny music have nothing to do with aggression against or contempt of his listeners but everything to do with a search for a way of expressing what he wants to express. And, what is more, that may affect the members' attitudes to some of the great composers of the past: even Beethoven was a human being! Some clubs and music societies have reported increased interest in their *classical* concerts after such an opportunity to meet and communicate with a real-life composer. The means by which a music club can achieve such ends must be many and varied. The vital thing is for clubs to try. Without such a direct meeting of minds—composer, performer, listener—at a personal grass-roots level, our musical scene will dry up: "museums" of early music, delightful though they may be in moderation, become an arid form of escapism from real life if they become the concert-goer's staple diet'.

Your club can also help by including works by living composers in a club's season of concerts and by including illustrated talks by composers in clubs' seasonal programmes.

Conductors: It is possible to assist them to some degree by large clubs engaging an orchestra to be conducted by a rising young conductor.

Music Teachers can be greatly helped as can their students if even one of the 'O' or 'A' level set works can be included in club programmes (depending on feasibility). Syllabuses are known far enough ahead to plan this though it will still be dependent on the artists having the works in their repertoire or being willing or able to learn them in time. Open and school clubs are best suited to help in this way.

FOSTERING FUTURE GENERATIONS OF MUSIC-LOVERS AND CONCERT-GOERS

Professional music making in public in its present wide scale will only last as long as there are those to promote it and attend the concerts or recitals. It is most important, then, that clubs, wherever possible, should do all they can to help instill into our young the love of music and concert-going. Again, open and school clubs are best suited to do this. Offer low priced junior subscriptions or non-member tickets to encourage whole families or school groups or classes to attend your concerts. If your venue is too small for this to be economically viable, do your best to promote occasional concerts especially for children from local schools of all kinds, for which grants may be available from local education authorities. Certain artists, ensembles and orchestras are geared to giving daytime schools' concerts which they repeat—adjusted —for adults the same evening at special all-in rates.

BRINGING PEOPLE TO MUSIC

Though clubs may promote superb concerts and attract the initiated by the horde, they will not be facing up to their full responsibilities unless they also reach and bring as large and broad a spectrum of music lovers as they can to that music. For hidden among us is a large, scarcely tapped reservoir of potential concert-goers: the diffident ones who are literally afraid to join a club because they believe—sometimes not without reason, I regret to say—

51

that we are still a tight-knit, condescending circle of musical highbrows, or have the odd belief that they cannot, therefore, be musical, much though they love music, and so are not qualified to join a club or go to a concert.

I often meet both these reactions and as often explain that there is nothing to fear or that if they love music of course they are musical, and in either case there is nothing to stop them joining a club or going to a concert, No one could have upheld this opinion more vehemently than Dame Isobel Baillie with whom I discussed this problem. Indeed, she believes that far too much fuss is made about 'understanding' music; that people are made to feel inadequate if they do not, and that all the pleasure and enjoyment of music is thus taken out of it for far too many. There are also those who have never given much thought to 'classical' music or believe they are only capable of enjoying light music or jazz. They can and do change their minds.

Is it worth bothering about these people? A thousand times YES. Surely they are the people clubs *should* be bothering about if they are to serve their public well.

THE MUSIC CLUB'S ROLE IN SUPPORT OF AMATEUR ORCHESTRAL AND CHORAL SOCIETIES

In order to ensure the continued supply of fine musicians and performances it is important for music clubs to support the amateur performing societies for in certain ways they are just as vital to the profession as the concert promoting clubs. Both orchestral and choral societies provide training grounds for conductors, help composers by commissioning new works and performing them, and provide experience for future professional orchestral players, instrumental soloists and solo singers. The choral societies also act as employers of professional and semi-professional orchestras, and providers of work for all professional solo singers in the great choral works, performances of which would virtually cease without such societies.

Concert-promoting clubs should, then, make every effort to draw attention to amateur performing societies' events by displaying their publicity at their own concerts and by free inserts in their concert programmes wherever space and timing of each others' events permits. Clubs should also allow the sale of tickets for the amateur performers' events at their own concerts where practical; there should be reciprocal arrangements for club publicity and ticket sales.

THE MUSIC CLUB'S ROLE IN COUNTERACTING GENERAL AUDIENCE SHORTFALL

Music clubs can do more than anyone else in this field, and indeed they must. Their very nature gives them the power (open clubs especially) to do a great deal to counteract the shortfall, being experienced at so many concerts, by direct and indirect means.

Direct Means
(a) By organizing coach outings to professional symphony and chamber orchestral concerts and major recitals, chamber music and choral events in London and elsewhere throughout the British Isles. Travel subsidies may be available from RAAs (see Appendix 2). Most professional promoters offer reduced rates for block bookings. The bother of booking and travel is taken from the concert-goer's hands, and such outings provide a great treat for older concert-goers and for the disabled for whom public transport or driving is impossible.
(b) By displaying at their (club) concerts publicity of at least some of the London or provincial symphony and chamber orchestras' concerts, major recitals etc.

Indirect Means
It is at local level, while making every effort to build their own memberships and audiences that clubs will automatically help to increase attendances at the major orchestral concerts and recitals. For I am convinced that they can do a tremendous amount throughout the country. If each person on, say, a ten-man committee recruits five new members, you produce fifty possible additions to audiences further afield. And if all open clubs—there are at least 375 listed—repeat the exercise, then it begins to make sense. Getting on for 19,000 newcomers to the concert-going world are not to be sneezed at. Also, though some you approach may not join your club, they may still, thanks to your efforts, attend some of your concerts and those further afield. In a while things begin to snowball, so that there is no reason why between you all the figures should not run into hundreds rather than tens of thousands of new concert-goers: no mean contribution towards counteracting the general audience shortfall and preserving our great musical heritage. The more you build your memberships and audiences the more you will do for music and therefore for your members and the public.

Committee and club members should call on newcomers to the district. Such approaches are always appreciated and new members often drawn into the fold, for belonging to a music club is one way of getting to know people. You must tackle personally those who keep meaning to join but never get round to it. Arrange to call on them and give them club literature; if nothing happens after a fortnight, phone.

Contact the elderly, the non-drivers, the lonely who won't venture out alone but all of whom are otherwise keen. Try to arrange transport to concerts for them; tell them how important their membership or concert-going is to the music world, and that they are needed. The singletons and the recently bereaved may be keen but too shy to join. They need to be convinced of the friendliness of your club, of the music world's need of their support, of the tremendous help they will be—if they have cars—by giving lifts and being responsible for getting people to concerts. These are the people who will respond to being involved. The diffident need to be reassured that they won't be out of place, but in like company; that probably the greater number of members are neither very knowledgeable about or performers of music and that this does not spoil their enjoyment of the music but enhances it, by actually seeing it being made and learning quite a lot from the programme notes.

The lovers of light music, jazz etc. must not be ignored. Often it needs just the right concert, be it chamber music, orchestral or a recital to hook them and set them exploring.

Be warm and welcoming. Any sign of condescension will put people off. Remember that you are working to destroy the reputation for snobbishness attached to music clubs, to open a new world to many people, and to increase support for your club and for the whole music world. You may wonder if you are supposed to be running a social welfare society rather than a music club. I can only reply that music is a great healer and soother; a great unifying force of people in all walks of life who enjoy, revel in and explore the same thing under the same roof and that, if by serving humanity we can also serve music and the profession or if by serving music and the profession we can also serve humanity, then these are the things we should be doing.

3. FOUNDING AN OPEN MUSIC CLUB

This must be set about in a very positive way. Whatever the size and type of club you have in mind your project is no small undertaking. If it is to succeed you must impress from the beginning. There must be no vagueness. It is no use having this wonderful idea, stirring up excitement and enthusiasm, only to find that there is no suitable venue or there is too much competition to make it a viable proposition. (See Feasibility Check List, Appendix 5.) You must be able to propose something that is feasible with every chance of success if gone about in the right way. You will then stand a greater chance of obtaining sponsorship and co-operation from those who can do so much to further your cause such as the press, local trades, business men etc., and of arousing a large, favourable response from the public.

1. Before approaching others likely to support your venture ensure there is a suitable venue.
2. Arm yourself with as much useful data as is relevant, including a copy of the NFMS draft model constitution and other NFMS information,

whether or not you intend to affiliate in due course. You are going to have to provide convincing arguments and answers when proposing your project and will create a far more favourable impression if you produce your evidence on the spot. (See Appendix 6)

3. Approach the editors of local papers and county magazines. Win their interest and co-operation.

4. Sound out people who could be in favour of the project—friends, known music-lovers, musicians, music teachers and so on.

5. Arrange an informal meeting of representatives of the press, your county magazine, local radio; the vicar and members of the parochial church council if you will be using your church, and of anyone else keen to support you, at which you:

   (a) discuss what the aims, objects and policy of the intended club should be, bearing in mind the role it should play in relation to its members, the neighbourhood and the music profession and to that end rough out a draft constitution and rules based on those of the NFMS draft model constitution, or use that draft, whether or not you intend to affiliate;

   (b) decide how to cover initial costs (see Finance, page 6);

   (c) decide how to sound out the public and 'sell' your project. There must be nothing haphazard here, for whether your club becomes a reality or not will depend on how large an initial response you can achieve. The most usual ways of doing this are by either calling a General Public Meeting at which the proposed club is explained, discussed and if the response in favour is large enough the procedure for forming the club is begun, or by promoting a Trial Concert, followed a week or two later by a General Meeting to which the whole audience and any other interested people are invited and the project outlined.

Finding a Patron or President

Before going ahead with whichever method you choose, remember that right from the beginning you must create and put across the image of a club to be proud of, with taste, which will promote fine concerts performed by fine artists at varying stages in their careers, a club for all music lovers and not specialists only, which will fulfil its obligations to members, the neighbourhood and the music profession. The greatest prestige you can give your club is to bless it with a Patron or President renowned in the music world. If, before your Trial Concert or General Public Meeting, you can announce that a distinguished person has agreed to become the club's Patron or President this is headline news for your local papers, thus guaranteeing bigger, better publicity. It also provides a great draw, as a sure sign of a club of substance and high standards with which people will want to identify and be associated, and far more people are likely to attend the

General Public Meeting or Trial Concert. So much the better if your Patron or President elect can manage to be an active rather than passive figurehead who may, if a performer, give his or her services free at the Trial Concert; attend the General Public Meeting to add weight to your arguments for founding the club; or if not a performer, give an illustrated talk on music matters; attend occasional club concerts and events; occasionally put you in the way of engaging an artist at a lower than usual fee.

How to find your Patron or President? (a) Artists' agents will be able to tell you who might be interested. (b) A suitable candidate may live in your district or have originated there. (c) One of you may know of someone or know someone who does. (d) Or simply be bold and write to whoever you like (see British Music Year Book/ISM Professional Register). If you are unable to find a suitable person, prestige can be given by using distinguished artists in your Trial or Inaugural Concert. They may even be willing to give their services for love or reduced fees to help launch the club. It is good publicity for them, but never expect this of them. But, prestige is not derived from big names alone. With them must go good taste. There must be nothing shoddy in the presentation of concerts or the running of your club. Ponder all this well before going ahead.

1. FOUNDING A CLUB BY MEANS OF A GENERAL PUBLIC MEETING

Before the Meeting
(a) Publicity: Such a meeting must be widely advertised and the publicity excellent for you will not have the bait of a Trial Concert. All the more reason for finding a Patron or President of repute whose name can be blazoned forth on leaflets, in the press and through all possible media including word of mouth.
(b) Book the venue—anywhere easily reached and convenient such as a village, church or school hall etc. preferably where refreshments can be served afterwards.
(c) Have ready the rough draft of the consitution and rules remembering that if you wish to become a registered or recognized charity these should be as suggested in the NFMS/SAC model constitutions as applicable. Also have ready all the useful, relevant information you have gathered. (Appendix 6)
(d) Choose the speakers, distinguished if possible, who must 'sell' your proposed club with convincing and authoritative arguments.
(e) Make arrangements for refreshments after the meeting.

At the Meeting, procedure will be much the same as for any General Meeting called to sound people out with regard to forming a society and then setting its formation in motion.

(a) Elect a chairman capable of controlling the meeting.

(b) Your speakers then explain and talk about the proposed club.

(c) Everyone then discusses it.

(d) If the favourable response is large enough, set the necessary procedure in motion for putting the proposed club on a proper footing. Resolutions as to the name, nature and objects of the Club must be proposed, seconded and voted on. If passed, move on to reading the draft constitution including any suggestions that may have been made during the Meeting's discussion. The Meeting then appoints a Provisional Committee to draw up the Constitution and Rules in the approved manner for submission at a second General Meeting which will be called by the Temporary Secretary. Ensure that at least one of the Provisional Committee is well versed in committee work and procedure.

No time should be lost in drawing up the Constitution and Rules as the real business of the Club cannot begin until it is properly set up. At this first General Meeting, the Temporary Secretary should take the names of all those wishing to become Founder Members together with as many subscriptions as possible (for which receipts should be given) if the rates have been fixed, and I strongly recommend that they should be. Subscription rates may either be nominal, and concert serial tickets at special rates paid for on top of that (see Appendix 1) non-members paying full rates; or they may cover the entire cost of admittance to all main concerts and possibly other events. I recommend the latter arrangement which assures you better returns, for it can happen that having paid a nominal subscription a member may not buy tickets for all the concerts.

(e) Any Other Business

 (i) Organize a competition for the best designed, appropriate logo for the club for use on stationery, posters, leaflets, programme covers etc. It is important for a club to have an insignia by which it is readily identified (see illustration page 77).

(ii) Discover Founder Members' talents, with an eye to a place on the properly constituted committee which will be elected at the Second General Meeting, or to helping with publicity, stewarding etc.

(iii) Ask Founder Members to think up ideas for the concerts and other club events for your first season for discussion at the Second General Meeting after the official business of putting the club on a proper constitutional basis is concluded.

(iv) Exhort Founder Members to spread the word and recruit more Founder Members. It is vital that members should be immediately and truly involved in the building of their club and not just the committee.

Second General Meeting. Before this is held and bearing in mind the make-up of a purposeful committee and what you have learnt by way of members' talents, sound out those you feel most suited to serve on the committee with regard to their willingness to be nominated, first ensuring that they realize just what they are undertaking if elected.

The Second General Meeting, called by the Temporary Secretary, should be held as soon as possible after the Provisional Committee has drawn up the constitution and rules. All Founder Members and any others wishing to join should be notified at least ten to fourteen days beforehand.

At the Second General Meeting the Constitution and Rules must be read out and passed one by one as they are submitted or after any alterations have been agreed, though the exact wording of the alterations (which can be difficult to settle on the spot) can be left to the committee for submission at the next General Meeting. *NOTE* The sooner that the Constitution and Rules can be finally ratified the sooner you can apply for registration or recognition as a charity. Now comes the election of Officers and the Executive Committee as laid down in your constitution.

And that's it. Your new club is born!

2. *FOUNDING A CLUB BY MEANS OF A TRIAL CONCERT FOLLOWED BY A GENERAL MEETING*

This method is on the whole preferable to the first for it gets to the nub at once by providing a sample of things to come. By choosing the right kind of concert, with the widest possible appeal to your particular district you are more likely to attract a greater number of potential members initially, even though a distinguished Patron or President has agreed to be present.

Stanley Weeden, the founder of the Three Rivers Music Society (Rickmansworth) used the second method with great success. A small steering committee, one of whom was a member of the local press recruited as PRO, was formed to organize and run the concert. A float and guarantee was provided by the founder/treasurer. A concert of the widest appeal was chosen—a Carol Concert with choir and orchestra to include audience participation at times. Application forms were enclosed in the programme brochures for those wishing to become founder members to fill in and hand over after the concert. The whole audience was invited to attend the General Meeting after Christmas at which, if the favourable response was large enough, the machinery would be set in motion to form the club. The concert was a sell-out, the steering committee swamped with requests to join at once and there was no question of not going ahead to put the club on a proper constitutional footing at the General Meeting. Founder Members totalled 250.

Founding a club after a Trial Concert follows the same procedure as detailed above. The first General Meeting must be given plenty of publicity after the Trial Concert as not everyone who may wish to join may have been able to attend that concert. It is also important to ensure that there are reviews of the concert which include information about the proposed club and the general meeting, in all local papers. Running the Trial Concert is dealt together with that of an Inaugural concert and a Season's Concerts in the next section.

3. FINANCING THE FOUNDING OF A CLUB

(a) Initial costs. See Finance, page 6.
(b) Financing the Trial Concert which, because it must be an impressive occasion, could be on the expensive side. Because there will be a limit on what can be charged for tickets (see page 9) you may have to resort to seeking sponsorship or guarantees. Your persuasive powers must be at their greatest in making prospective sponsors or guarantors feel their importance in being in on the founding of a club vital to the district's needs and the music profession.

Grant Aid and/or guarantee from your RAA
(a) *For a Trial Concert* help might be forthcoming provided that you have a properly constituted committee and are prepared to submit audited accounts. Make enquiries at least nine months before the concert. Remember that programme content and proof of self-help can influence an award.
(b) *For an Inaugural Concert and rest of season.* See *Running a Music Club,* below.
    NFMS guarantees and other benefits are not forthcoming until a club affiliates. If this is desired, application for affiliation should be made after your first two or three concerts—if you feel the club will succeed—enclosing information about the club, its size, nature, constitution, copies of concert programmes and the season's brochure.

4. OFFICE MATTERS

Once your proposed club has become a certainty give thought to the smooth running of its office work. You will need loose-leaf files into which all dealings with artists, agents, venue managements, printers etc., can be put for easy reference; a file or files in which to keep the numerous artists' brochures, agents' and artists' representatives' lists; a membership file in which to keep records of all members.

4. RUNNING AN OPEN MUSIC CLUB

The running of a music club begins as soon as the club has been founded and consists basically of planning and preparing for the first season including the all-important Inaugural Concert; running the first season; simultaneously planning and then preparing for the second season, during the running of which you plan and prepare for the third season and so on and so on.

Club and Concert Management run in parallel as well as merging over common matters. Broadly speaking:

(a) *Club management* deals with the overall running of a club and includes planning seasons in keeping with its aims and objects; financial affairs; enrolment of members; running the AGM and any other general meetings; keeping records and membership files; applying for NFMS guarantees and other benefits, RAA/SAC grant aid and guarantees etc.; seeking sponsorship and donations; running fund-raising events, outings.

(b) *Concert Management* deals with every aspect of the promotion of all the professionally performed concerts from the very beginning.

(c) *Club and Concert Management* merge over publicity for the recruitment of members. After all, the CM depends on members to provide the greater part of the audiences. The running of members' events is also a joint affair between club and concert management if these events are concerts. Business dealt with at committee meetings is a mixture of club and concert management varying in proportion according to the time of year. For instance, during the concert season meetings will be concerned with running the current season, acting on the results of concert post mortems and planning and preparing the next season. As the season closes, they will be more concerned with the AGM and publicity to ensure the captivation of present members and the recruitment of new ones.

Planning a season
The planning of the first season is the same as for any other in that your goal must be to carry out the aims and objects of the club to the highest degree possible in the best possible way, by doing any or all of the following:
(a) Using popular concerts and big names to subsidise or go part way towards subsidising the all important young artists' concerts or less popular specialised concerts (see page 49);
(b) obtaining sponsorship, donations and other forms of assistance;
(c) planning programmes so as to gain (as appropriate) maximum NFMS guarantees/RAA/SAC grant aid or guarantees.
  The general aim must be to plan a season of main concerts and members' events sufficiently attractive and interesting to impel people to join the club, yet which, at the same time, will further the appreciation, knowledge and enjoyment of music. In the average season of five or six concerts you will need

60

to include at least three names of repute or three very popular concerts. This is especially important if you are within easy reach of London and working in competition with the South Bank or other major music centres. The pattern of main concerts should be to alternate well-known names and popular programmes with the less popular names and programmes. Begin with a bang. The first concert is vital and must attract as many people as possible in the hope that any non-members having sampled the club's workings and atmosphere, having seen the notices of the rest of the season in the concert programme on posters plastered around, and having studied the season's brochures (readily available at the concert), will wish to join then and there or as soon as they can reach their cheque books. It is just as vital to end the season with a bang and a packed house. For then you must aquaint everyone with the mouthwatering news, however brief, of what is planned for the following season. You may also wish or find it to your advantage to link your planning with local or topical events.

Programme selection—artists and works may be influenced by all or any of the following:
(a) the finding of members' preference through polls;
(b) cut-price tours offered by certain Regional Arts Associations, the Scottish or Welsh Arts Councils, some agents or by artists themselves;
(c) the previous season's programmes;
(d) anniversaries of composers' or musicians' births or deaths; Royal or important occasions;
(e) artists' fees, their drawing power;
(f) current competition winners, when slots are left in programmes into which a winner or finalist can be slipped.
A season's programme selection must be made with great care aimed at upholding your club's objects yet at the same time concocting an extremely attractive, well-balanced programme which will enhance your image and build up membership.

Remember that if your club is NFMS affiliated your treasurer must submit all programme details, details of artists, their fees etc. on the form supplied together with the current registration fee to the NFMS by the *30th April* each year in order to qualify for consideration of awards; that application for grant aid from RAAs towards cost of piano hire and/or for guarantees must be made before *30th August* each year; and that if you hope to promote a specialised programme of contemporary works or a series of concerts built round one composer and so on, this should be discussed with your RAA's Music Officer to see what help might be forthcoming *before* you actually go ahead with bookings.

Members' Events. While planning your season's main events thought should also be given to Members' Events if you wish to include these in your activities. These are the more intimate club activities for members and their guests which are slotted in between main concerts; they must also be open to the public in the case of registered or recognized charities. They may be held in members' homes, small hired venues or your main venue if suitable. They may be financed partly from the subscriptions and partly from entry charges for guests and members of the public, sale of refreshments, profit on a raffle etc. Such events might be anything connected with music including:

(a) concerts by members for members;
(b) illustrated talks by members, professional musicians, composers, conductors etc.;
(c) concerts by promising performers still at school but bent on professional careers;
(d) concerts by outstanding young artists just beginning their professional careers, especially rehearsal concerts for their London debuts (see page 48);
(e) rehearsal concerts by older young artists in preparation for a major recital;
(f) demonstrations, such as one given at Woking by the Susuki Group, London;
(g) concerts for young intending soloists in their final year at college or university.

Outings to concerts, opera, ballet, plays, exhibitions, festivals and in support of young artists at their major recitals in London and other major music centres should also be features of your club's activities.

The Annual General Meeting must be held within a limited time of the ending of your club's financial year according to your rules. Its date should be fixed for inclusion in your season's brochure.

Preparing for and running a season is much the same for the first or any season.

Advance publicity

Your PRO's job is to excite and hold people's interest in your club at all times. The end of a season is not a signal to ease off. During the hiatus between seasons the renewal of memberships must be secured and new members sought to bring in enough funds to cover not only early expenses but those of the greater part of the season well before it starts. Publicity for your next season must, therefore, start before the end of your current one or as far ahead as possible of a new club's first season.

An established club must get at least the names of artists and concert dates of its next season into the programme of the final concert of its current season at which there should also be posters (even if hand-done) showing dates, programmes where possible and members' events as far as planned. After the final concert the continuance of early publicity depends on how soon the next season's brochure can be printed. Try to have it ready for distribution when the chairman's letter is sent round notifying everyone of the AGM. If this is not possible on no account let publicity hang fire. Produce an *Interim Leaflet* to go out with the chairman's AGM summoning letter; have plenty at the AGM for members to take away; display them for take-away in libraries, music shops etc. and urge committee members to carry some around (see page 16). New clubs should also make use of such leaflets as soon as possible before the start of their first season. *Contents of an Interim Leaflet*. (See Appendix 7.)

Exhibitions of photos of all artists taking part, their programmes, photos of the club in action etc., are excellent and most rewarding incentives to recruitment staged at intervals between the AGM and start of the season or before the start of a new club's first season. There must also be advance press releases of news of the coming season or first season as soon as details are settled including acknowledgement of any sponsorship. (See page 17.)

Membership Cards should be printed well in advance of the coming season so that new and rejoining members are not kept waiting too long after enrolment or rejoining. It is useful if the briefest programme reminder is printed on the back of these cards.

Fieldwork. The run-up to any concert is a busy, exciting time but even more so for the opening one of a season, an Inaugural or a Trial Concert. So very much hangs on their success. There must, then, be an enormous push in the field, starting, at the latest, four weeks before these concerts. Posters must go up, leaflets be distributed along with the season's brochures and you must talk, talk and talk. Where possible, *all* committee members should carry and sell non-member tickets once the members' priority booking period is over. For a Trial Concert such ticket selling is vital.

Be generous with complimentary tickets at the Trial, Inaugural and Opening Concert of any season. In the long run it may well pay many times over. As well as the press, invite your Patron or President, sponsors, guarantors, the mayor, other local dignitaries, the Music Officer of your RAA, an NFMS officer, someone from your county magazine and other people who could become interested in helping your club and don't forget the artist's traditional couple for relatives or friends.

Press reviews, diary entries, exhibitions, radio and general publicity, see pages 16–18.

It can also be advantageous to hold a reception after your Trial or Inaugural or opening concert for those who matter both to the club and artists. It does not need to be an ostentatious affair but does round the thing off very well and makes for plenty of goodwill. There is no reason why small receptions should not be held after all concerts for that matter, with a small charge for refreshments. Indeed many clubs do arrange this, if not at the venue at a committee member's home. If the sponsors themselves do not arrange for a post-concert reception then a club should arrange for this so that the sponsors, committee and artists can meet.

Photographs. For the Trial, Inaugural and any especially important concerts try to arrange for photos to be taken. Your club must make news in the next issue of your local paper and photos help enormously. If possible there should be photos when a concert is sponsored. Keep copies for your archives. They can also be useful in exhibitions. If you want photos of a concert in action remember to ask permission of the artists, the venue management and, if agreeable, ensure that very few photos are taken. Constant flashes irritate audiences though artists are trained to cope, and will be glad of the publicity.

Tape recording of Inaugural or other concerts. (See Tape Recording of Concerts, page 29.)

Concert Programme Brochures. While artists are being engaged and programmes agreed, decisions must be made as to the form your concert programme brochures should take remembering that they have to do the same two jobs as your season's programme brochure (see page 21 and Appendix 8).

Covers for an Inaugural Concert's programme should be rather special to encourage everyone to buy a copy as a souvenir of the club's founding.

Concert Day Arrangements
You should provide:
(a) a well-signed and situated table where new members can enrol, enquiries be made and club literature obtained;
(b) notice boards for your own posters, those of other music societies and musical activities both local and further afield;
(c) somewhere where RAA literature and any other take-away literature can be displayed;
(d) somewhere where tickets for the next concert can be bought either before the concert, during the interval or after the concert or at all three times, as convenient;
(e) an exhibition of photos of artists appearing at the rest of the season's concerts and their programmes.

At all times make an especial effort to create an intimate, friendly and welcoming atmosphere. All committee members and officers should wear brightly coloured, easily seen badges and go out of their way to talk to members and non-members, doing their best to encourage the latter to join. It is important to take note of audience reactions and store all comments for concert post mortems. Immediately before the start of a concert your Patron, President, chairman or some other spokesman should, from the platform, give a warm welcome to everyone, make any *brief* announcements to do with the club or special events, draw attention to news in the programme, then announce and warmly welcome the artists.

After concerts it is a great help to the treasurer if the concert manager can feed him or her the figures, i.e. the total number of seats occupied, the number taken by members, non-members and the number of complimentary seats; returns on the sale of programmes and refreshments (if provided by the club). As the season progresses you soon see which type of concerts are most popular and which must be sponsored or guaranteed if you are to continue promoting them.

Members' events. Treat these more as social occasions by allowing ample time for refreshments and talk among members and those giving the entertainment when this is over. If the event is held in a hired venue give it a welcoming atmosphere with flowers about the place. The ice can be broken by holding a raffle, say for a record token, which at the same time helps to raise funds. Again, try to have somewhere to display your own publicity, other interesting literature and other societies' coming events, as well as copies of your season's brochure very much in evidence for guests or members of the public, and the wherewithal to enrol them if they wish to join.

Remember, if these events are open to the public the venue must either hold a *Music, Singing and Dancing Licence* or be adapted to conform to the regulations governing the issue of an Occasional Licence—if in an area where this is required.

The Annual General Meeting, though not the most popular of events, is, nevertheless, an extremely important occasion and every effort should be made to lure as many members to it as possible by gaining a reputation for conducting it in a well-run businesslike manner which allows plenty of time for a social evening afterwards. For, it is at AGMs that the committee accounts for its doings, members can air their grievances, give praise, make suggestions or alter and amend the constitution and rules. It is at AGMs that the financial statement is explained and the club's financial transactions approved, or not, by its members; committee members can be voted off the committee if members disapprove their actions, and officers and committee members be re-elected or replaced.

Your AGM must be called formally, usually by a letter from the chairman to all members not less than a certain number of days before the meeting (as set down in the rules), in which there must also be a request for nominations of members willing to stand for election as officers or committee members according to the rules for replacing them from time to time. It is usual to include in the letter a brief report of the club's doings, brief details of the coming season (or enclose an interim leaflet), the proposed subscription rates a plea for cheque books to be brought ready for renewing membership and an enrolment form if you are not enclosing an interim leaflet with one attached. There should also be information as to the entertainment being offered after the AGM. This may be simply wine and refreshments with time to talk to friends, or may also include a short musical diversion by members or young musicians.

The inclusion of a club report in the chairman's letter cuts down the time spend on the AGM as it can be taken that everyone has read it. Keep postage down by delivering as many of these letters as possible by hand, enlisting the help of members. Or, as some clubs do, have these letters ready in their envelopes laid out in alphabetical order for members to pick up at the last concert of the season. The AGM is also an ideal occasion for the PRO to speak about the club; to ask for volunteers for a poster-putting-up-leaflet-distribution team; and to inspire them to be as determined as the committee to build a flourishing, go-ahead club which is not only the talk of the town but of the music world. Make your AGM work in every possible way for the good of your club.

There is tremendous satisfaction in making your club successful and its presence well and truly felt. But remember that this can only be achieved and maintained by a tremendous amount of hard work, vision, boldness, common sense, full use of the personal approach, excellent team work; by never being satisfied and constantly striving for improvement. No matter how successful the Trial, the Inaugural or any concert or any season, there must be no resting on your laurels or the whole thing will start to fall away. You will be contending with a constant turnover of membership, and people will not join or attend concerts as non-members if they don't know that your club exists. The news which travels the local grape vine must be of a club that does all in its power to promote as high a standard of concerts as possible in as comfortable and congenial surroundings as possible. The news that travels the professional grape-vine (and it does) must be of a club which really cares for the artists and takes its responsibilities to the music profession seriously.

Always remember that a club cannot be run casually in odd spare moments. From my own observations and experiences and those of many others, it is only too obvious that the clubs which really thrive are those blessed with one or more committee members who, as well as being utterly dedicated, have the organizing powers, go-getting ability, enterprise, determination and the energy, drive, initiative and the time to make their club succeed: those who refuse to be daunted or beaten. Otherwise the going is hard indeed.

66

5. RESURRECTING A MUSIC CLUB

By now you should have a pretty good idea of why your club died, is ailing or tottering on the brink. Before you can set about putting new life into or recreating a club you must first, in the light of this book, take a ruthlessly honest and critical look at yourselves to discover where you are falling down or why your club died. For, it is no use laying the blame on such adverse factors as the lure of TV, Hi-fi, Radio Three, London's South Bank or other major music centres, nor on an unsatisfactory venue, lack of interest, the dropping off of members due to old age, moving etc., adverse local financial climate and so on. You had and have it in your powers to overcome, or largely overcome, these obstacles instead of bowing to what you may believe to be an inevitable finale. Don't, though, expect an overnight miracle. It will take several seasons of concentrated battling when everything appropriate in this book must be thrown in and kept in action.

First, you must put your house in order. Until you have a good, purposeful committee you will get nowhere. If people have their club's survival at heart it is imperative for them to give way to progressive ideas and actions. What is needed is someone with business acumen, vision, imagination, a flare for PR work, drive and enterprise, who can give a club a new look, aided and abetted by a purposeful committee doing all in its power to assist selling it. Then, except in exceptional circumstances, there is every reason for you to make a comeback.

No move must be missed with publicity and PR. It is vital to involve members and former members in the fieldwork needed to revitalize or recreate your defunct club. If each member recruits only one new member they will double the size of the club just like that. Offer incentives to those recruiting the most new members. But, remember that no one is going to join unless you've got something very tempting to lure them with. Therefore choose programmes and plan seasons to work for and not against you. To start with they may have to consist mainly of very popular works with only the occasional unfamiliar or deeper piece slipped in. In areas where there is little competition it is a grave error to think that anything will do; that people are so starved for lack of live music that they will come to anything. They may once or twice, then give up.

Give your club a welcoming friendly image that does not frighten away. For instance, much though you may wish to bill a social event as a 'Musical Conversazione' *don't*. You immediately label the club as being a compact circle of highbrow specialists with whom the less knowledgeable will be afraid to join. Offer all possible personal service: lifts, getting people's tickets, giving information. Arrange to meet potential members, who ring up making enquiries, so that you can talk about the club and so on. Go all out for sponsorship, donations and other forms of help. Do everything possible to improve your venue if this is the cause of the trouble. You may find that the club's constitution needs revision.

But, whether recreating or revitalising a club, you must never rest in your efforts to keep it surging ahead and confounding the pessimists you are bound to come up against. It will take time and must be worked and worked at but it *can* be done. Then, having built a new and splendid reputation and image, see that the whole depressing business does *not* begin all over again.

6. THE SMALLER, DRAWING ROOM-TYPE PRIVATE CLUB

Founding such a club is done by word of mouth and circularising all those who might be interested, to inform them of the proposed club and invite them to a meeting to discuss the possibilities of going ahead. Matters for discussion should include:

(a) *concert venues*—whether to be held in various members' homes, in only one private residence or all in a small hired venue. A ruling factor here will be the use of as good a piano as possible, (preferably a grand though it need not be full-sized) for any concerts needing a piano;

(b) *the size of the club*—membership may exceed the seating capacity of venues by a certain amount, as rarely will all members attend each concert;

(c) *seating*—chairs can be hired but in the long run it may pay to buy your own, the sort that stack. You will need somewhere to store them between concerts and suitable transport if concerts are to be held in different houses. The initial outlay of buying chairs could be covered with donations or by holding a private fund-raising event. It may also be possible to recoup some of the outlay by hiring your chairs out. Another solution is for everyone to bring their own chair, though if of varying height and size they may not fit in as well as those of a uniform size and height;

(d) *objects of the club*—even for small private clubs these should be based on those of the NFMS draft 'model' Constitution—(with the public element excluded) for they have the same responsibilities to their members and the music profession as open clubs;

(e) *admission to the club* should be by recommendation only, new members to be proposed and vouched for by those recommending them;

(f) *subscription rates and admission prices for guests* should be based on what you feel members can afford while at the same time taking into consideration the cost of the concerts and administration;

(g) *covering initial expenses* (see page 6);

(h) *types of concerts*—when deciding on what sort of concerts you hope to promote, the important role of small private clubs in relation to the music profession should be remembered, and a resolution made that only really outstanding young performers be used whether still at school, college or university or starting their professional careers as well as established artists if and when this can be managed;

(i) *'Music, Singing and Dancing Licence'* (see page 27).

Once it is decided to go ahead, the procedure is much as that set out on page 54 (excluding the public element). Regardless of its smallness and excluding the public element, small private clubs should be run very like open clubs. There should be the same care over programme content and looking after artists. If a piano is being used it should be tuned, preferably on the day of the concert. Artists can be obtained through the same sources (see page 30). If supplying refreshments, this must be organized to run smoothly, and so on. *NOTE* Because seating capacity will be very limited, members should be asked to inform the relevant committee member, and in good time, whether they will be attending a concert or not so that if there are seats to spare anyone wishing to bring a guest can be informed. At concerts a list can be made of those wishing to attend the next one at the same time stressing that if subsequently anyone cannot attend they should give notice of this as soon as possible. The same rules about tape recording of concerts apply as to open clubs, see page 29. The season's brochure and concert programmes should be as comprehensive as possible. But because your resources may be small and you are not having to sell your club, duplicated sheets will suffice. The season's brochure should include dates, times, venues, artists, cost of subscriptions and an application form for joining the club. Concert programmes should include the names of the artists, the works to be performed with their movements/parts etc., and, if possible, brief notes on the works, though it is more usual at these more intimate concerts for the artists to talk about the works instead. If it is possible to include short biographical notes on the artists so much the better. The interval should also be indicated, and a note of the next concert. Outings should be run from time to time to other musical events and members encouraged to attend concerts promoted by nearby open clubs, especially those given by artists who have previously performed at their own club. An AGM should be held at the end of your season with some form of entertainment to follow and refreshments.

7. SCHOOL CLUBS

1. Founding a school *open* club may follow the methods detailed above for founding open clubs but with modifications to suit particular circumstances. For instance, when publicising your intentions, circularize as appropriate and according to type of school: the governors, parents and pupils, teaching, administrative and domestic staff, friends, and others likely to be interested, as well as using the other publicity methods to reach the public. Or, if you wish to limit membership to pupils, staff etc., and only admit the public as non-members at the doors before concerts, make this clear in your publicity. The objects and constitution of school clubs should be those of the NFMS draft model constitution, for their responsibilities are the same as those of non-school open clubs and there is the same need to become a registered or recognized charity. Affiliation to the NFMS should also be seriously considered to enable the promotion of works and artists. Arrange to have the use of the school's duplicating facilities, or, where the school curriculum includes a secretarial or printing course, let the advanced pupils be responsible for all duplicating and printing. Indeed, the older pupils of senior schools *should* be involved in the founding of their school club, for the experience of forming and getting an organization under way, if for nothing else. Let them attend the general meetings, design advance news posters and leaflets, deal with the press, help distribute publicity and so on. Let senior music students write the programme notes, art students design programme covers, others prepare the programme copy, write the previews, organize teams of programme sellers and stewards and so on for the Trial Concert.

A school club should have as purposeful a committee as a non-school one. The fact, especially where boarding schools are concerned, that you have a captive audience does not mean that anything will do. The same importance should be attached to projecting an image of a well-run, caring, go-ahead club as with a non-school club. You have an example to set and the goodwill of parents and public to win. The larger the membership and the more non-member tickets sold, the more you can do to widen your pupils' musical enjoyment, knowledge, appreciation and experience and the more you can do for the music profession. Be sure that this is understood at the club's inception.

Running a school open-club should be much the same as running a non-school open club but with modifications to suit particular circumstances. Wherever practical involve pupils as much as possible; although financial transactions and actual booking of artists must be done by adults, let them see how this is done. Ensure that they understand the importance of the club to themselves, the public and the profession and how they can be instrumental in helping to further the careers of old pupils in training as professional performers or trying to establish themselves as such.

Programme content should be chosen with especial care, to create a life-long love of music and concert-going while at the same time stimulating the exploration of music and its appreciation and the appreciation of its fine performance. The amount of publicity needed will depend on how many of the public there will be room for after seating the 'captive audience', and other members. The fewer the spare seats the less the publicity required and vice versa. Concert management should be as efficient as for a non-school club concert with the same attention to detail, including the understanding care of artists. Non-member tickets may be sold at the door or by advance sales either through the school or by shops etc. acting as agents, or by committee members.

2. Founding a school *private* club is done by circularising as appropriate the governors, parents, teaching, administrative, domestic staff and others connected with the school to inform them of your intentions and invite them to a meeting to discuss the proposed club. If you decide to go ahead the procedure is much the same as above but without the public element. The club's objects should be based on those of the NFMS draft model constitution (excluding the public factor) for its responsibilities should be the same as an open club's to its members and the profession, and to this end the club should be set up with the same purposefulness and pupil involvement as for a school open-club.

The running of a school private club is the same as for a school open-club but without the public element, any publicity being purely a private, internal matter, and admittance to concerts being by subscription or members paying for guests.

Outings should be organized by School Open and Private Clubs to symphony chamber orchestras' concerts and great choral performances etc. to broaden their pupils' musical horizons and let them experience concert-going in the true concert environment of our major concert halls.

SINGLE SCHOOL CONCERTS

Where it is impossible to form a school club it is important that occasional professionally performed concerts should be promoted if at all possible, for the benefit of pupils and the profession. Such concerts can be run either as public or private concerts—if private, run as a concert promoted by a school private club, if open as a concert promoted by a school open club. In both cases there should be as much pupil involvement as is possible and practical. Agents will advise about artists and ensembles who give concerts especially for schools, often at reduced rates for a daytime concert if it can be repeated the same evening for a nearby promoter. It may be possible to obtain a grant towards the cost of such a concert (private or otherwise) from your local education authority. For a school public concert it may be possible to obtain aid from your RAA/SAC.

All schools, with or without clubs, who boast ex-pupils who have since become outstanding young musicians trying to establish themselves can render no greater service than by offering them engagements, especially as try-out concerts before their debuts or other major recitals or appearances. It should be the policy of schools to ask such ex-pupils to keep in touch with them and let them know when they can best be of any help in this way.

In *all* concerts to which the public is admitted, make sure you obey the requirements of the *Music, Singing and Dancing Licence* regulations.

8. INSTITUTION MUSIC CLUBS

Founding an open or private university, college, hospital, bank or other institution music club is done in much the same way as founding a school open or private club but with modifications to suit the institution, though the same objects should be pursued as in the NFMS draft model constitution, private clubs excluding the public elements. Open clubs in this category should also consider affiliation with the NFMS to enable them to pursue their objects conscientiously, for they are as vital as any other club to the music profession for the benefit of their members. Publicising the proposed club and general meeting to discuss its formation should be done by circularising all staff, students, directors, lecturers, doctors, nurses etc. and postering all departments, offices, wards, staff-quarters etc. as appropriate. The regulations concerning *Music, Singing and Dancing Licences* (page 27), tape recording of concerts (page 29), Performing Right (page 28) must be observed.

In running an institution's club you should pay special attention to internal publicity. All faculties, departments, offices, wards or staff quarters should be postered, and announcements made on the tannoy, if available: persuade the powers that be of the very real necessity for this. I have been to hospital concerts where the attendance has been poor due to lack of efficient publicity organization and to college concerts in public venues where the low turn out was obviously due to lack of external and internal publicity.

The amount of external publicity needed will depend on the institution, and how many members and non-members can be depended on for attendance from the internal publicity.

72

Notice boards displayed at a concert giving prominence to forthcoming events and activities of other societies, both local and further afield.

The Concert-Promoting Music Festival

There is no more excellent reason for holding a music festival than for the sheer joy of bringing fine live music to your neighbourhood and, if held in a church, to the glory of God. However, such events mean a considerable upheaval in a church's normal running and unless the idea stems from the church you may need a more concrete reason with which to win over the clergy and parochial church council: perhaps to celebrate a royal occasion, as was done in Chobham for the 1977 Silver Jubilee, or to commemorate the birth or death of your church's patron saint, a great churchman or musician, or to aid a good cause or charity. Indeed, most of the original festivals such as the Birmingham, Norwich or Three Choirs festivals were pioneers in this field. Because country roads were impassable during the winter the original festivals were held in the summer or early autumn and generally speaking today's are also held during those months. (Incidentally this solves one of the problems of complying with the regulations governing the issue of M, S & D Licences, as, provided the concerts are during daylight hours, you will not need to provide emergency lights.) In the past, only sacred music was allowed in sacred buildings; today, however, orchestral and chamber music concerts are permitted, though anything lighter such as a Viennese or Gilbert and Sullivan evening may have to be found another venue.

Music festivals play an important role in the professional music world. They were and are occasions for which new works were and are commissioned, and there is no reason why smaller parish festivals should not follow suit. Festivals also play their part in furthering the careers of outstanding young artists by devoting at least one concert or recital to one or more of them. Festivals also provide employment for established and distinguished artists as well as for orchestras of all sizes, and for professional singers with amateur or professional choirs. Nor should youth or school orchestras be ignored if of sufficiently high standard.

At one time, festivals or music meetings as they were often known, were only associated with major ecclesiastical centres where they were well patronized by city businesses and the county families. At the same time they were eagerly looked forward to and became traditional features of English provincial life and social events of considerable standing, as indeed they are today. But now they are also being based on parish churches in village and town and it is with these smaller, local festivals, which could also become a traditional English feature that this part of the book is concerned.

PLANNING AND RUNNING A MUSIC FESTIVAL

Planning and preparing a Music Festival follows much the same lines as those for planning and preparing a music club's season, in that there are a series of concerts to plan, after which the concert manager directs all operations connected with the mounting and selling of the concerts.

First explore the feasibility of your project (see Appendix 5) in good time so that, this being satisfactory, you will still have at least a year from the start of your planning until the start of the festival.

NOTE: Your local choral society or amateur orchestra will, should you wish to use them, need at least a year's notice (if NFMS affiliated) for them to be able to work your date in with their programme.

1. *Form a properly constituted, purposeful committee:* properly constituted because, if it is a non-profit-making festival you may be eligible for RAA aid or guarantees (see Appendix 2). Because your festival is a parochial affair you will know and be able to draw on church groups, the Women's Institute, floral and art clubs, staff of local schools and so on for committee members and helpers as well as for advice on where to borrow things and who has the required expertise.

2. *Before the first committee meeting* have to hand all the relevant facts (see Appendix 6).

3. *First Committee meeting*
(a) Decide on the number of concerts to be promoted. Play safe for a first-time festival: better three or four rewarding concerts that can be run really well than more which might over-tax finances, your stamina and man-power. Feel your way with a first festival. Use it to gain experience and gauge the general reaction.
(b) decide the nature of the concerts bearing in mind that:
 (i) they will be held on consecutive days;
 (ii) if all of the same type, say string quartets or choral works, only one kind of audience will be attracted, many of whom may not be able to afford or be free to attend more than one concert;
 (iii) your aim must be to attract capacity audiences;
 (iv) you should be catering for as wide a field of music lovers as possible.
(c) work out a provisional budget (see page 5) in order to determine what you will have to spend on artists. Do not base your budget on a sellout of tickets and programme brochures. Remember that only the professional element in amateur orchestral or choral concerts is likely to be considered for RAA aid, also that people tend not to want to spend so much on going to an amateur performance as to a professional one;

(d) choose the artists and alternatives so that if the first choice falls through you can carry on booking without having to refer back to the committee. Local performing societies using professional soloists should be included;

(e) choose programmes (see page 18) remembering that though you may have preferences for certain works this is something that cannot be settled until the artists have been approached. If commissioning a work arrange this as soon as possible so that it will be finished in time for the artists to learn it. Contact your RAA for advice about this and possibly obtaining a grant to help cover the commission fee;

(f) decide how to cover initial expenses (see page 5);

(g) discuss the possibility of other attractions, such as an exhibition of local or church history, or of ecclesiastical embroidery etc.; discuss whether to make it a combined music and flower festival: form the appropriate sub-committee;

(h) decide whether to have a patrons' or stewardship scheme;

(i) settle where the Festival Box-Office should be, ideally it should be easily seen and accessible.

Generally speaking, the management of a festival's concerts is the same as for any concert. The Concert Manager should allocate, as appropriate, the various tasks to be undertaken by committee members, and committee meetings should be held from time to time for progress reports.

Festival Brochure. A special design should be created for the brochure cover which should be arresting enough together with the brochure's contents to encourage its sale as a souvenir even to those not wishing to attend the concerts. For contents see Appendix 9, but also note that at least half the brochure should be sold as advertising space, to cover all printing costs. Local shops and businesses are usually keen to support such an event. Ask customers to settle their accounts with their orders—a splendid way of bringing in early revenue. Remember to supply them with a free copy of the brochure as soon as it is printed.

Ticket Selling. Apart from a Festival Box-office, also arrange for shops and businesses in your own village or town and nearby to act as ticket and festival-brochure selling agents and to display posters and leaflets. If agreeable to the shop or business management, arrange for committee members or others to stimulate ticket and brochure selling at these sales points.

Publicity. (See page 15.) Also make full use of your parish magazine and those of neighbouring parishes if possible. Persuade the clergy or their wardens to display posters and leaflets in their church porches and halls, and to call attention to your festival when giving out notices during services. For details of items to go on posters and leaflets see Appendix 7.

WOKING

MUSIC

CLUB

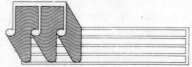

THREE RIVERS MUSIC SOCIETY
(Affiliated to the National Federation of Music Societies)
President : The Chairman of Three Rivers District Council

HORBURY CONCERT SOCIETY

Primrose Hill Road, NW3

Patron: Sir Peter Pears C.B.E.

A selection of music club logos.

Do your best to involve everyone in your village or town, regardless of their denomination, to do their bit towards making the festival a success. The big push and run-up to the festival starts in earnest two or three weeks before the first concert. It is now that *all* committee members and helpers should be either manning the box-office, stimulating ticket and brochure sales at other sales points, or be out and about armed with tickets and brochures. Remember that every ticket sold in advance is one more safeguard should the weather be foul or something crop up to prevent or deter people from coming at the last moment. Throughout the run-up the treasurer should collect and bank all takings each day and arrange for the use of a night safe for the takings on each night of the festival.

A few days after the festival hold a post-festival Committee Meeting to hear the final accounting and decide whether to continue promoting festivals at intervals, remembering that if it is to be annually you should be getting down to the next one straight away. If, however, you are thinking in tri- or biennial terms, then something must be done with the cash balance, such as putting it on deposit with the bank who dealt with the festival current account. Income Tax will have to be paid on the interest. However, if the festival is to become a regular event and not in aid of charity or profit-making, it may be possible to register it or have it recognized as a charity when you would be exempt from paying tax. Seek advice from your RAA/SAC. The auditing of the accounts should be arranged as soon as possible after the festival, especially if you are receiving aid from your RAA.

By going about your festival practically and making every possible use of the personal approach all should go well. Who knows? After a time your festival may become nationally famous. But what really matters is that you should bring live music to your parish by means of a festival to the glory of God and for the joy and enrichment of His people and the benefit of music and those who make it.

SECTION IV

The Single Concert

Whether public or private, single concerts are promoted for various reasons: to support a charity or a good cause; to further an artist's career; to celebrate an occasion; to commemorate the birth or death of a great musician; as a memorial to someone; to give school instrumentalists, singers, orchestras and choirs the chance of performing to an audience; to encourage the cultural growth of school children and inspire young school musicians by occasionally engaging professionals to perform for them; or simply for the sake of bringing music to people. They are most valuable in providing employment for the professional musician and in helping outstanding young musicians.

First, explore your project's feasibility (see Appendix 5), and the possibility of obtaining aid from your RAA/WRAA/SAC, which could be especially valuable if promoting a concert for an outstanding young artist or if you need to hire a piano or other keyboard instrument. If all is well, go ahead, remembering that you will need a properly constituted committee if you wish to obtain such aid. Seek these organizations' advice about this. Initial expenses may be covered as suggested above (page 5) and sponsors, guarantors and donations sought, especially for a charity concert when your aim must be to hand over as large a sum as possible to that charity. It may be to your advantage not to have tickets but an 'Admittance by Programme' arrangement, whereby programme brochures are sold at a price to cover the cost of a seat and the programme. With this arrangement seats are not numbered, and printing costs reduced.

NOTE: Charity and private concerts are *not* eligible for WRAA/RAA/SAC aid.

Programme Content: For a charity or good cause concert the works should be very popular and the artist well-known. Some are willing to lower or even waive their fees for such concerts in which case you should pay their expenses. For a concert given in the furtherence of an artist's career, leave the choice of works to them. If they are using it as a rehearsal for a London debut or major recital then obviously they will be playing the works in that programme at your concert.

Publicity: Information on posters and leaflets will vary according to the type of concert (see Appendix 7).

Press Previews: (a) For young artists using your concert as a rehearsal for their debut, as well as including the usual biographical notes stress that the programme will be the same as at that important appearance on such and such a date.

(b) For charity or good cause concerts emphasise the charity or good cause, and if the artist is giving his or her services free, acknowledgement of this should also be included.

Previews for all types of single concerts should be accompanied by photos. Programme brochures will vary according to type of concert from (for a charity concert) the ideal, booklet form in which you sell masses of advertising to cover costs and benefit the charity, to a single sheet if it is a young artist's concert run on a shoestring when all that matters is for that concert to happen, in which case, though not ideal, the artist can always talk about the works.

For concerts featuring little-known, up-and-coming artists you must work especially hard to get a worthwhile audience. But it is possible. A great deal of ticket selling must be done personally by the committee and others. You need great belief in the artist, which you must be able to put across. Explain the importance of giving an artist a good audience and how vital the experience is to their career. Leave no stone unturned. Nothing should be ignored which can make the concert a success for the artist and to cover costs. That is not to say that you should not go all out for all types of single public concerts, but for the unknown artist you must somehow do even more or you will not get that audience.

Charity and good cause concerts:

(a) seek all the sponsorship, donations and other forms of help that you can. The latter could be called hidden or invisible sponsorship or donating taking the form of low cost printing, free flowers, reduced piano hire and so on, all of which must be acknowledged in the programme and, with luck, in the press, which repays the donors with free advertising;

(b) make a collection either during the interval or at the end of the concert and make sure that there are enough collectors so that no one is missed;

(c) after the concert, the press and main supporters should be notified of the amount you were able to hand over to the charity or good cause;

(d) as with any other sponsored concert, the sponsors should be thanked by letter.

NOTE: For all concerts, make sure you enforce the laws on Performing Right (page 28), tape recording (page 29) and obtain a Music, Singing and Dancing Licence if necessary (page 27).

ORGANIZING AND RUNNING A SINGLE PRIVATE CONCERT

These concerts may be as large or small as wished or can be managed; held in hired venues, an institution's premises or a private residence. Admission is by invitation only and in the form of a subscription. Concert Management is as for a concert promoted by a private music club.

Ticket table with forward booking facilities and future event literature.

The National Federation of Music Societies (NFMS)

(In this context Societies = Orchestral and Choral Societies. Clubs = Concert Promoting Clubs)

It is essential to be aware of the considerable advantages—financial and otherwise—afforded to open clubs and societies by their affiliation to the NFMS. Inaugurated in 1935 the NFMS's aims and objects as set out in the Memorandum of Association, are, broadly speaking 'to maintain, improve and advance education by promoting the art and practice and the public performance of music throughout the United Kingdom and in other countries'. This general aim naturally embraces many subsidiary aims which include:

1. Providing central and regional organizations for the purpose of securing the mutual assistance of clubs and societies.

2. Administering a scheme of Financial Assistance to help clubs and societies to improve their standards by the employment of professionals. This is operated by means of funds provided by the ACGB for clubs and societies in England and by the SAC in Scotland. Welsh Societies are aided through the WAMF, with funds from the WAC. In the form of a guarantee against loss the aid is intended to improve the standards of societies' performance and clubs' promotions, the amount being related to the fees and expenses payable to the professionals taking part.

NOTE *In Scotland,* the NFMS only awards guarantees to societies, the concert-promoting clubs receiving theirs via the SAC. Nevertheless, many clubs do affiliate in order to obtain the other benefits.

In Wales, societies may be affiliated but receive grants and guarantees from the WAMF only (with WRAA help) and whereas promoting clubs may be affiliated to the NFMS none are.

Applications are submitted by affiliated clubs and societies on the appropriate form available from the General Secretary of the NFMS by 30th April each year in respect of the following season. The aid offered must be acknowledged in prescribed terms, in concert programmes.

'Offers of aid in England are decided by a Joint Allocation Committee representing the NFMS and the ACGB, and in Scotland by a Joint Committee representing the NFMS and the SAC. Overall administration of the whole scheme is in the hands of the General Secretary of the NFMS, who also acts as Secretary of the Joint Allocation Committee.

'NFMS members needing subsidy should also apply for aid to their RAA, Local Authority (and neighbouring Local Authorities if part of their audience is drawn from the neighbourhood) and to their local Education Authority. Various enactments permit these bodies to help if they wish.' The size of guarantees is subject to the discretion of the Joint Allocation Committees and it would seem that the more a club or society can implement the aims and objects of the NFMS, the more enterprising their programmes and the more self-help by way of sponsorship and fund-raising they can manage, the larger their guarantees are likely to be. Clubs and societies incapable of or unwilling to make such efforts may find their guarantees cut back, very small or non-existent.

3. Organizing schemes for exchange of orchestral and choral music.

4. Running a scheme of insurance, at the best rates, covering public liability, abandonment of concerts, and instruments belonging to societies.

NOTE If you 'go it alone' you may find it impossible to obtain insurance cover for abandonment of concerts except at very high rates.

5. Running a scheme giving clubs and societies cover against payment of performing right fees on the repertoire of the Performing Right Society (PRS) for concerts held in halls not holding PRS licences.

6. Arranging conferences and meetings. The annual conference is a most valuable event to which all affiliated clubs and societies should send at least one delegate, preferably the Federal Representative (FR) as only he or she may vote. It is a great 'swap shop' of learning how others solved problems similar to yours or vice versa. News of especially outstanding young artists is passed on, as it is of those not thought so much of. At the same time the NFMS is keen to know how members are faring with agents, artists, local authorities, hall managements, their RAAs and so on, so that if possible the NFMS can take up any difficulties on behalf of those in trouble. There are also workshops and talks covering many aspects of performance and promotion. For the same reasons, regional NFMS meetings should also be attended by at least the FR.

7. Negotiating terms with the Musicians' Union, the Music Publishers' Association and so on for the benefit of affiliated members.

8. Operating a Piano Loan Fund. (See page 26).

The NFMS is one of the organizations who jointly made the document concerning *The Copying of Music and the Copyright Law* between composers, publishers and users with regard to graphic copying which includes photocopying of music, and is one of the bodies to whom requests should be addressed in cases where a user and a copyright owner are unable to agree on the interpretation of any part of this code (see Appendix 11). Working with a very small but efficient staff and the aid of its equally efficient Executive Committee the NFMS gets through an immense amount of work for the benefit of its affiliated members and is constantly on call for them to take their problems and troubles to.

Advice on founding a club wishing to affiliate can be had from the General Secretary, who can also supply a copy of the draft for a 'model' Constitution for a club or society which it is advisable to follow in England and Wales as being the most likely to satisfy the Charity Commissioners for the purpose of registering your club or society as a charity. Clubs wishing to affiliate should consult the General Secretary and, on application, send him a copy of the constitution, copies of recent programmes, season's brochure and other relevant matter. New clubs should *not* apply unless sure that they can keep going.

A Federal Representative (FR) must be appointed as soon as the club is accepted for affiliation. In law, it is the person who holds the post who is the member of the NFMS rather than the club or society represented. Complete the relevant form received when making enquiries and return it to the NFMS when you apply for membership. In due course your FR may be elected to your Regional NFMS Committee, later to the NFMS Council and perhaps to the Executive Committee.

NFMS Guidance on seat prices. 'Members of the audience must pay adequate prices for seats for concerts for which aid is requested. Few clubs could manage if they charge only the minimum laid down by the Joint Allocation Committee. However, offers of aid to societies which do charge less than the minimum may well be lower than that which might be merited by the quality of the concert. The following minima apply:

Serial tickets (subscriptions) should be priced so that the average cost per concert is not less than the sum currently stipulated. Single tickets should be priced so that non-members cannot attend more than two-thirds of the concerts for a total outlay less than the cost of the serial ticket/subscription. Concessionary seat prices may be offered to senior citizens and full-time students.'

For all further details and the NFMS Register of Members and Handbook apply to the General Secretary, The National Federation of Music Societies, Francis House, Francis Street, London SW1P 1DE (tel. 01 828 7320).

(Quotations are from the NFMS handbook and other literature by kind permission of the General Secretary, John Crisp).

APPENDIX 2

Regional Arts Associations (RAAs), The Welsh Amateur Music Federation (WAMF) and The Scottish (SAC) and Welsh (WAC) Arts Councils

RAAs cover virtually all of England (12) and WRAAs all of Wales (3) (see addresses below page 89) and have been created to foster, develop and promote the arts in their regions including by means of financial aid. They are supported by funds allocated by the Arts Council of Great Britain (ACGB), the WAC, local authorities, and wherever possible by financial assistance from industry, businesses, trusts, private patronage and members' subscriptions. Each region has its own constitution and policies which, where the promotion of music is concerned, may vary from region to region and country to country though certain matters are common to all. For instance, financial aid is only given for the promotion of *public non-profit making* concerts and musical events and, generally speaking, for the professional rather than the amateur element.

The SAC forms part of the ACGB whose objects are:

1. To develop and improve the knowledge and understanding and practice of the arts.
2. To increase the accessibility of the arts to the public throughout Great Britain.
3. To advise and co-operate with Government departments, local authorities and other bodies on any matters concerned directly or indirectly with these objects.

The SAC's work is largely concerned with the subsidising of professional arts activities to which the public has access.

Promoting organizations in Scotland should contact the Music Director of the SAC for information about financial aid.

Financial aid from the above sources can be as a Direct Grant, a Guarantee against loss or a Subsidy. *But, none of this aid is yours by right.* Awards are only made on the observance of certain conditions (see below) common to all RAAs/WRAAs *and* subject to the discretion of their Music Advisory Panels. *In Scotland* each application to the SAC is considered on its own merits; the Council's response in every case is guided by the recommendation of the Music and Dance Committee. NOTE: Scottish music clubs, even if NFMS affiliated, should apply to the SAC for financial assistance. *In Wales* there are at present no NFMS-affiliated clubs, their aid being channelled in the main through the three WRAAs. It is possible that in future links will be made between the WAMF and music clubs.

Financial aid may be given as:
1. *Guarantee against loss to any non-profit making promoter of public musical events other than English NFMS-affiliated music clubs except in certain circumstances for:*
(a)   the performance of new, contemporary or little or unknown older works, a series

of concerts devoted to a particular composer etc. which are not likely to draw large enough audiences to prevent a loss;

(b) performances by exceptionally outstanding but as yet not well-known young artists for the same reason as in (a).

2. *Direct Grants to all non-profit making promoters of public concerts whether NFMS/WAMF affiliated or not, for:*

(a) covering part of the costs of hiring pianos or other keyboard instruments. NOTE Applicants to the SAC should include this item as part of their estimated concert expenditure;

(b) the commissioning of new works.

3. *Travel Subsidies* to your concerts from places within your region or to transport members of your organization (private or otherwise) to events within your region. NOTE The SAC does not arrange subsidised travel to concerts. Transport subsidy schemes partially funded by the SAC are operated by Scottish Opera, the Scottish National Orchestra, the Scottish Philharmonic Society and the Edinburgh International Festival. Some Scottish Music Clubs and Arts Guilds operate transport subsidy schemes, the cost of which they write into their annual revenue applications to the SAC for financial assistance. *RAAs/WRAAs, the SAC/WAC/WAMF* (addresses below) will supply you with Notes on the Guidance of Applicants for the above aid and all other relevant information.

Other Types of Help
1. *Co-ordination of Artists' Tours*
(a) *In England* this service is at present provided by the Northern Arts, Lincoln & Humberside Arts and South West Arts for all public-concert promoters.
(b) *In Scotland* the SAC's Tours Department co-ordinates arrangements for tours of artists of ensembles, which have been requested by a number of promoting bodies in Scotland. The Tours Department itself has no subsidiary function. No special financial subsidies accrue to organizations booking events co-ordinated by the Council. An annual tours' circular is issued by the Tours Department. It contains a non-selective list of artists seeking engagements in Scotland.
(c) *In Wales* there is at present very little co-ordination of tours by individual artists around music clubs, basically because they are at present regionalized. It is hoped this may be remedied in the future by the re-introduction of regional and national planning conferences.

Artists inform the co-ordinating bodies of the dates when they will be available for, say, four to ten consecutive days and what their fees will be, according to the number of bookings obtained during that period. The co-ordinators then circularize all promoters of public concerts, musical events or festivals as to which artists are available and when, and possible programmes. Then, in most cases, they arrange a conference in the autumn for interested promoters to attend and discuss what is being offered and as it were, make their bids. Matters are then taken from there by the co-ordinators. This service may make the difference between being able to afford certain artists or not and it is a pity that more regions do not offer this service, for it is becoming increasingly difficult for amateur promoters, especially the smaller clubs, to engage any but the lower fee artists. Obviously such schemes are complicated to operate and clubs are notoriously independent as to what they want, but it *is* being done successfully and artists and agents wish that much more could be done in this field. Promoters should keep pestering their regions until something is forthcoming.

2. *Promotion of Young Artists*
Annual schemes promoted by RAAs to help young artists at the beginning of their careers which also benefit concert promoters, include:

(a) *The South East Arts Association (SEAA) 'Young Musicians' Platform'* provides a valuable Wigmore Hall concert and subsequent engagements in the SEAA region and elsewhere. Competitive, but avoiding the invidious situation of choosing an overall winner (max. age 30), the scheme instead selects four musicians who receive the same benefits and kudos. The SEAA promotes these artists by acting as their agents in negotiations and in offering special incentive guarantees against loss to promoters engaging any of the winners, NFMS-affiliated clubs included (details from SEAA).

(b) *The Greater London Arts Association (GLAA) 'Young Musicians' Scheme'* is now established as an important link between the most promising young performers and concert promoters in the Greater London Area. Selected from a series of auditions, artists are given concerts at the Purcell Room which promoters can attend with a view to offering future engagements. The GLAA emphasizes that its role is as a shop window and not an agency. The particular advantage of this scheme is that promoters engaging Young Musicians for concerts in the Greater London Area can apply for grants towards the artists' fees. Funding from the Arts Council of Great Britain and generous donations from London Weekend Television make this scheme possible (details from the GLAA).

3. *Other Subsidised Schemes Promoted by the Arts Council of Great Britain or by RAAs/WRAAs*
(a) Contemporary Music Network Tours throughout the country which are promoted and subsidised by the ACGB (details from the ACGB Music Department).
(b) Appearances of ensembles resident at certain universities which are sought, organized and subsidised by the RAAs in the regions in which the universities are situated, such as the Leonardo Piano/String Trio resident at Hull University (Lincolnshire & Humber Arts), the Fitzwilliam String Quartet at York University (Yorkshire Arts) and the Chilingirian String Quartet resident at Sussex University (South East Arts Association).

4. *Advice.* The Music Directors and Officers of RAAs/WRAAs/SAC/WAC/WAMF are there to give advice on the forming of organizations for the promotion of public concerts and festivals etc., on artists, programmes, the feasibility of your proposed music projects and so on. Don't hesitate to make full use of their services.

5. *Symposia* are arranged by some RAAs including SEAA, from time to time on subjects useful to their concert-promoting members.

6. *Free Advertisement in Diaries.* All RAAs/WRAAs publish diaries of musical events in their regions. They are sent periodically to all RAA/WRAA members which include

Libraries, Civic Centres, Arts Centres, Music Clubs, Societies etc., and are also available to non-members for a small sum. *In Scotland* the SAC produces *Rostrum,* the SAC Calendar of performances given either directly or indirectly with financial support from the SAC, which is distributed throughout Scotland. (Apply to the relevant organizations for copy dates and the special forms to complete with details of your events.)

7. *Assistance with buying pianos* (See page 26)

8. *Public Pianos for hire* (See page 25)

9. *Provision of Model Constitutions for Organizations wishing to obtain Charitable Status in Wales and Scotland.*
In order to obtain charitable status an organization's constitution must be so worded and framed as to be deemed charitable by the Charity Commissioners and Inland Revenue in England and Wales and the Inland Revenue in Scotland—no easy task. To save difficulties for those not using the NFMS model constitution, Draft Model Constitutions have been prepared to take care of this in Wales where no clubs, as opposed to orchestral or choral societies, are NFMS affiliated, and in Scotland where, in any case, you are safer in using the Model prepared by the SAC. Scottish music clubs should send their constitutions to the claims branch of the Inland Revenue in Edinburgh to check that they are acceptable for non-profit-making organizations. *Model Constitutions* are available from the WAC/WRAAs/WAMF and the SAC who will inform you where to send your application to become a registered charity (England and Wales) or a recognized charity (Scotland).

THE ARTS COUNCIL OF NORTHERN IRELAND (ACNI) (Not connected with the ACGB)

While the ACNI has been responsible for the formation of 26 Arts Committees linked to each district Council and these bodies are extremely active in promoting all types of artistic endeavours, not least the sponsoring of visits by the Ulster Orchestra and solo recitalists to provincial centres, there is not the same music club system as in the rest of the U.K. However this does not mean that such a scheme might not eventually come about and anyone now inspired to found such a club or promote a non-profit making festival should not hesitate to approach the ACNI for advice and even possible financial aid.

THE ARTS COUNCIL OF GREAT BRITAIN 105 Piccadilly, London W1V 0AU (tel: 01 629 9495)

SCOTTISH ARTS COUNCIL 19 Charlotte Sq., Edinburgh EH4 4DF (tel: 031 226 6051)

WELSH ARTS COUNCIL Holst House, Museum Place, Cardiff CF1 3NX (tel: 022 394711)

ARTS COUNCIL OF NORTHERN IRELAND 181a Stranmillis Rd., Belfast BT9 5DU (tel: 0232 663591)

THE ARTS COUNCIL, EIRE 70 Merrion Square, Dublin 2, Eire (tel: Dublin 764685)

REGIONAL ARTS ASSOCIATIONS

EASTERN ARTS ASSOCIATION 8–9 Bridge St., Cambridge CB2 1UA (tel: 0233 67707)
(Bedfordshire, Cambridgeshire, Essex, Hertfordshire, Norfolk, Suffolk)

EAST MIDLANDS ARTS Mountfields House, Forest Rd., Loughborough, Leicestershire LE11 3HU (tel: 0509 218292)
(Derbyshire (excluding High Peak District), Leicestershire, Northamptonshire, Nottinghamshire, Milton Keynes District of Buckinghamshire)

GREATER LONDON ARTS ASSOCIATION 25–31 Tavistock Place, London WC1H 9SF (tel: 01 387 9541/5)
(The area of the 32 London Boroughs and the City of London)

LINCOLNSHIRE & HUMBERSIDE ARTS Saint Hugh's, Newport, Lincoln LN1 3DN (tel: 0522 33555)
(Lincolnshire and Humberside)

MERSEYSIDE ARTS ASSOCIATION Bluecoat Chambers, School Lane, Liverpool L1 3BX (tel: 051 709 0671/3)
(Metropolitan County of Merseyside, District of West Lancashire, Ellesmere Port, Halton Districts of Cheshire)

NORTHERN ARTS 10 Osborn Terrace, Newcastle upon Tyne NE2 1NZ (tel: 0632 816334)
(Cleveland, Cumbria, Durham, Northumberland, Metropolitan County of Tyne and Wear)

NORTH WEST ARTS 52 King St., Manchester M2 4LY (tel: 061 833 9471)
(Greater Manchester, High Peak District of Derbyshire, Lancashire (except District of West Lancs), Cheshire (except Ellesmere Port and Halton Districts)

SOUTHERN ARTS ASSOCIATION 19 Southgate St., Winchester SO23 7EB (tel: 0962 69422)
(Berkshire, Hampshire, Isle of Wight, Oxfordshire, West Sussex, Wiltshire, Districts of Bournemouth, Christchurch and Poole)

SOUTH EAST ARTS ASSOCIATION 9–10 Crescent Road., Tunbridge Wells, Kent TN1 2LU (tel: 0892 41666)
(Kent, Surrey and East Sussex)

SOUTH WEST ARTS 23 Southernhay East, Exeter, Devon EX1 1QL (tel: 0392 39924)
(Avon, Cornwall, Devon, Dorset (except Districts of Bournemouth, Christchurch and Poole), Gloucestershire, Somerset)

WEST MIDLANDS ARTS Lloyds Bank Chambers, Market St., Stafford ST16 2AP (tel: 0785 59231)
(County of Hereford and Worcester, Metropolitan County of West Midlands, Shropshire, Staffordshire, Warwickshire)

YORKSHIRE ARTS ASSOCIATION Glyde House, Bradford, West Yorkshire BD5 0BQ (tel: 0274 23051)
(North Yorkshire, South Yorkshire, West Yorkshire)

WALES

NORTH WALES ASSOCIATION FOR THE ARTS 10 Wellfield House, Bangor, Gwynedd LL57 1ER (tel: 0248 53248)
(Clwyd, Gwynedd and District of Montgomery in the County of Powys)

SOUTH EAST WALES ARTS ASSOCIATION Victoria St., Cwmbran, Gwent NP4 3JP (tel: 063 33 67530)
(South Glamorgan, Mid-Glamorgan, Gwent, Districts of Radnor and Brecknock in the County of Powys and the City of Cardiff)

WEST WALES ASSOCIATION FOR THE ARTS Dark Gate, Red Street, Carmarthen, Dyfed (tel: 0267 4248)
(Dyfed, West Glamorgan)

APPENDIX 3

Broadcasting & Television

BRITISH BROADCASTING CORPORATION

Head Office: Broadcasting House, London W1A 1AA (tel: 01 580 4468) (This number reaches all BBC staff in London)

Scotland Broadcasting House, Queen Margaret Dr., Glasgow G12 8DG (tel: 041 339 8844)

Wales Broadcasting House, Llandaff, Cardiff CF5 2YQ (tel: 0222 564888)

Northern Ireland Broadcasting House, 25–7 Ormeau Av., Belfast BT2 8HQ (tel: 0232 44400)

South and West Broadcasting House, Whiteladies Rd., Bristol BS8 2LR (tel: 0272 32211)

North New Broadcasting House, Oxford Rd., Manchester M60 1SJ (tel: 061 236 8444)

Birmingham Broadcasting Centre, Pebble Mill Rd., Birmingham B5 7QQ (tel: 021 472 5353)

BBC Television Music Section Kensington House, Richmond Way, London W14 0AX (tel: 01 743 1272)

BBC LOCAL RADIO

Birmingham B5 7SO (tel: 021 472 5141)
Blackburn BB2 2EA (tel: 0254 62411)
Brighton BN1 1TU (tel: 0273 680231)
Bristol BS8 1PP (tel: 0272 311111)
Carlisle CA1 2NA (tel: 0228 31661)
Cleveland (Middlesbrough) TS1 5DG (tel: 0642 48491)
Derby DE1 3HY (tel: 0332 3611111)
Humberside (Hull) HU1 3NU (tel: 0482 23232)
Leeds LS2 8NJ (tel: 0532 42131)
Leicester LE1 3SH (tel: 0533 27113)
Lincolnshire (Newport) LN1 3DF (tel: 0522 40011)

London W1R 0JD (tel: 01 493 5401)
Manchester M60 7BB (tel: 061 228 1991)
Medway (Chatham) ME4 4EZ (tel: 0634 46284)
Merseyside (Liverpool) L1 6BS (tel: 051 236 3355)
Newcastle NE2 1DZ (tel: 0632 814243)
Norfolk (Norwich) NR1 3PA (tel: 0603 617411)
Nottingham NG1 3BJ (tel: 0602 47643)
Oxford OX2 7DW (tel: 0865 53411)
Sheffield S10 2QU (tel: 0742 686185)
Solent (Southampton) SO9 4PJ (tel: 0703 31311)
Stoke-on-Trent ST1 1JJ (tel: 0782 24827)

INDEPENDENT RADIO

Independent Broadcasting Authority 70 Brompton Rd., London SW3 1EY (tel: 01 584 7011)

Programme Companies

Beacon Radio (Wolverhampton, all week) (tel: 0902 757211)
BRMB Radio (Birmingham & Midlands, 24 hours a day every day) (tel: 021 359 4481)
Capital Radio Ltd (London) (tel: 01 388 1288)
Downtown Radio (Belfast, all week) (tel: 0247 815555 sales; 0247 815211 news)
London Broadcasting Co. Ltd (London news and information all week) (tel: 01 353 1010)
Metro Radio Co. (Tyne/Wear, all week) (tel: 0632 884121)
Pennine Radio (Bradford, all week) (tel: 0274 31521)
Piccadilly Radio Ltd (Manchester, all week) (tel: 061 236 9913)
Plymouth Sound Ltd (Plymouth, all week) (tel: 0752 27272)
Radio City (Liverpool, all week) (tel: 051 227 5100)
Radio Clyde Ltd (Glasgow, all week) (tel: 041 204 2555)
Radio Forth Ltd (Edinburgh, all week) (tel: 031 556 9255)
Radio Hallam Ltd (Sheffield & Rotherham, all week) (tel: 0742 71188)
Radio Orwell Ltd (Ipswich, all week) (tel: 0473 216971)
Radio Tees (Teesside, all week) (tel: 0642 615111)
Radio Trent (Nottingham, all week) (tel: 0602 581731)
Radio 210 Thames Valley, Thames Valley Broadcasting Ltd (Reading, all week) (tel: 0734 413131)
Radio Victory (Portsmouth, all week) (tel: 0705 27799)
Swansea Sound Ltd (Swansea area) (tel: Gorseinon 893751)

INDEPENDENT TELEVISION

Addresses of regional companies available from IBA (see above)

APPENDIX 4

Competitions for performers in the UK

(A detailed list with addresses of the promoters is in the British Music Year Book)

Anderson (Emily) Prize for Violin Playing. Age 18–30. Irregular.
BBC Piano Competition. Max. age 30. Irregular.
Benson & Hedges Gold Award for Singers. Max. age 35. Annual.
Flesch (Carl) International Violin Competition. Max. age 30. Biennial.
Imperial Tobacco Cello Awards. Max. age 30. Biennial.
Leeds International Pianoforte Competition. Max. age 30. Triennial.
Leeds International Competition for Musicians in association with Pianoforte Competition. Max. age 30. Triennial.
Lionel Tertis International Viola Competition. First held in 1980.
Mozart Memorial Prize for Performers. Max. age 29. Biennial.
NFMS Award to Young Concert Artists. Annual, for various instruments and voices in rotation.
Royal Overseas League Music Festival. Max. age 25. Singers. Annual.
Teyte (Maggie). Singers. Max. age 30. Biennial.
Young Welsh Singers. Max. age 30. Triennial.

There are also competitions promoted by the ISM for older artists who have come late to the profession.

The SEAA and GLAA promote competitions, see Appendix 2.

APPENDIX 5

Feasibility Check List

Matters to be considered before deciding whether or not to go ahead with your project.

1. The suitability of the venue (see page 10).
2. Whether the proposed venue's seating capacity is sufficient to make the project a viable undertaking.
3. The availability of the proposed venue.
4. Whether the venue is already licensed, or complies with or can be adapted to comply with the regulations governing the issue of a *Music, Singing and Dancing Licence* required in most regions for premises in which such entertainments are held (see page 27).
5. Whether the hiring fee for the venue is reasonable or if you can come to a reasonable agreement with its managers. (In many cases local authority halls offer special terms to non-profit-making organizations. If yours does not, then do your best to change matters. You will have the support of other local organizations and a concerted drive by all of you could do the trick.)
6. Whether there will be any serious competition, by way of other concerts, festivals, clubs or societies, major local or national events, exam sittings and so on, as appropriate to your proposed project.
7. Availability, if required, of your local orchestral or choral society for your proposed project. NOTE Most of these societies plan their seasons' programmes at least one to two years in advance.

APPENDIX 6

Items and Data to Assemble (as appropriate) For First Committee Meeting when Founding a Music Club, Running a Festival or Single Concert

1. *Of Venues under consideration:*
    (a) Capacity, acoustics, box-office facilities etc.
    (b) Hire rates: possibility of special rates.
    (c) If holds M S & D Licence, a PRS Licence and Public Liability Insurance.
    (d) If a 'Public Piano' is available for use in situ.

2. *From Your RAA/WRAA/the SAC* (as appropriate)
    (a) Copy of policies re specific art forms.
    (b) Copy of notes on Guidance on Applying for Grant Aid etc.
    (c) Cost of WRAA/RAA membership: application form for same.

3. Full Information about the NFMS, whether intending to affiliate or not.

4. The ISM's Professional Register of Artists.

5. From Agents, their lists of artists (See Appendix 12).

6. From various printers/duplicating firms: approximate costs of the printing or duplicating you are likely to need.

7. Cost of Public Liability Insurance other than via the NFMS.

8. Information about Performing Right and cost of PRS Licence other than via the NFMS, from the Performing Right Society, 29–33 Berners St., London W1P 4AA.

9. Information about M S & D Licence if proposed venue not so licensed.

10. Availability of piano on loan and cost of moving and insuring same.

11. Cost and availability of piano for hire.

12. Cost of insuring piano via NFMS or otherwise.

13. Information on becoming a registered or recognized charity from the NFMS/SAC/WAC, your RAA as appropriate, and copy of their model constitution.

14. Copy of the Code of Fair Practice with regard to the graphic copying of music including photocopying, from the ISM or NFMS.

15. Firms, businesses possibly interested in sponsorship, guarantees and donations.

16. Any other information which you feel could save time and allow a preliminary budget to be worked out at the first committee meeting.

APPENDIX 7

Check list of Information which must be included on posters or leaflets

It is all too easy to leave out a piece of vital information. Check that you have included:

1. Date/s, Time/s and Place/s of Concert/s.
2. Name of promoter/promoting organization.
3. Price/s of tickets/subscriptions: where available: when available.
4. Address for postal sales, with request for use of SAE. Telephone number of box-office and/or enquiries.
5. Title of concert if it has a title: e.g. Celebrity Concert, Recital, Concert in aid of ...., or the .... Music Festival.
6. Names of chief artists, their instrument or voice.
7. A clause to allow you to alter the programme or artists if necessary, and a statement acknowledging co-operation with local council or by kind permission of, or whatever is appropriate.
8. Programme, i.e. composer, work and catalogue number (if one). NOTE: If the programme consists of many items it may be better to include only one or two in detail, then say 'and works by ....' and list the rest of the composers.
9. Posters advertising a club's season should also include information about the club i.e. subscription rates, where to apply for membership, where enquiries can be made, whether members have priority booking.
10. The number of the club's season. i.e. fifty-seventh season.
11. Registered Charity No. .... (if registered), or Recognized Charity (Scotland).
12. And of course the Club's Name and Logo.

APPENDIX 8

Contents of a Club's Season's Brochure

(A) *ESSENTIAL CONTENTS*

Outside cover
(a) The name and style of the club.
(b) Club's logo.
(c) Patron's and/or President's name.
(d) Which season.

Inside
(a) Fixtures, their dates, times, artists, venues and acknowledgement of use of venue/s where necessary.
(b) Dates when members' priority booking and public booking opens.
(c) Ticket rates for members if not included in subscriptions. Ticket rates for non-members and where and when obtainable.
(d) Information about the club: subscription rates, what they cover, where to apply for membership; members' privileges; name, address and telephone number for enquiries.
(e) Obligatory acknowledgements as appropriate to NFMS/WRAA/RAA/SAC for financial or other assistance.
(f) Acknowledgement of sponsors, guarantors and any other assistance.
(g) Small map of venue's whereabouts if hard to find.
(h) Statement reserving the club's right to alter programmes and artists.
(i) Application form for membership.
(j) List of committee.
(k) If appropriate, statement that the club is a registered charity (give number) or a recognized charity in Scotland.
(l) A few words about the role of music clubs in the music world and an appeal for people to use this brochure to spread the word about the club and recruit new members. This is most important.

(B) *OPTIONAL CONTENTS*

Any of the following can be added to the above.
(a) Brief notes on artists.
(b) Photos of artists.
(c) List of artists who have appeared in the past.
(d) Any other apt information.
(e) Advertisements to offset costs.
(f) List of Patrons; how to become one (if you operate such a scheme).
(g) Information about other societies' choral or orchestral events. This can be reciprocal and builds goodwill and each others' audiences.

(C) *IDEAL CONTENT:*

All of (A) and as much of (B) as is applicable or possible.

The more information that you can pack into these brochures and the more of them that you can have the better they will serve you.

CONTENTS OF CONCERT PROGRAMME-BROCHURES

(A) *ESSENTIAL CONTENTS*

(a) Venue, time and date of concert (if not on cover).

(b) Artist/s, their biographical notes however brief, prefixed with something like, 'It is a great pleasure to welcome ....'

(c) Works to be performed, their movements, composers and their dates (in correct order of performance).

(d) Notes on each work.

(e) Indication of the interval, its duration and if refreshments are available.

(f) News of club's forthcoming events, rest of season. When priority and public booking opens for next concert.

(g) Club information, i.e. subscription rates, privileges of membership, how to join, whom to contact for information etc.

(h) Acknowledgements as appropriate and required of assistance from the NFMS/WAMF/WRAA/RAA/SAC.

(i) Acknowledgement as appropriate of other guarantees, aid or sponsorship.

(j) Warning about the tape recording of concerts.

(k) A request for people to use the programme to spread the word about the club.

(l) An exhortation for people to join the club during the interval.

(m) If at all possible from time to time short editorials on the role of clubs and their members in the music world and news of any major engagements or performances of outstanding young artists who have performed for you. In fact, treat the programme brochure in part as a magazine or news letter.

(n) From time to time include information on the work done by your WRAA/RAA, the NFMS/WAMF/SAC as appropriate.

(B) *OPTIONAL CONTENTS*

Any of the following may be added to the above.

(a) Photos of the artists.

(b) Fuller biographical notes of artists.

(c) Fuller information about the club and coming events.

(d) News of other local choral or orchestral societies' events with possible reciprocal arrangements.

(e) Advertisements to offset costs, apart from those on cover.

(f) 'For sale' or 'Wanted' small advertisements might also be inserted to do with things musical at little or no cost to members or non-members.

(C) *IDEAL CONTENTS*

All of (A) and as much of (B) as possible.

NOTE For a club's Inaugural Concert the content should include as much as possible of the above and very definitely a paragraph or two about this auspicious occasion and what the club hopes to attain.

For a Trial Concert with expectations of leading to the founding of a club, omit (f), (g), (m), (n) in Section (A) and (c), (d), (f) in Section (B) and insert information about the proposed club, a request for people to come to the general meeting to form the club, and to encourage others to come. Also an acknowledgement if any artists have given their services to make the concert possible. There should also be information on where further information can be obtained and a detachable or a separate application form for those wishing to become founder members.

If sponsors are present at any club, trial or inaugural concert a welcome should be accorded to them in the concert programme, and they should be given the chance of including a message therein.

APPENDIX 9

Contents of Festival Programme-Brochure

Normally, to save expense, these are designed to carry full information about each concert so that they can be used as programmes at each concert.

(A) *ESSENTIAL CONTENTS*

On the cover or top outside of folder: name and style of Festival, price of brochure and a suitable design.

Inside
(a) Names of committee.
(b) Price of tickets, where obtainable by post and otherwise; opening dates of advance and normal booking.
(c) Acknowledgement of use of church, school or other venue
(d) If there is also to be an exhibition of flower arrangements, the venue's history and so on, give times and places and other information. Also list exhibitors, exhibits, flower arrangers, their arrangements, etc., if possible.
(e) Biographical notes of artists, choir, orchestra and conductor as appropriate.
(f) Programme of each concert, its date, time, venue and price.
(g) Programme notes for each concert.
(h) Indication of interval, its duration and if refreshments are available.
(i) If orchestra, the names of conductor, leader, players and their instruments.
(j) If choir, the names of directors, singers, their voices.
(k) Warning about tape recording of concerts.
(l) Acknowledgement of RAA assistance if any.
(m) Acknowledgement of sponsorship, guarantors, etc.
(n) List of patrons or stewards (if any).
(o) Statement reserving right to alter programmes and artists.
(p) Advertising.

(B) *OPTIONAL CONTENTS*

Any of which can be added to the above:
(a) An editorial about the Festival including any exhibitions.
(b) Illustrations to the editorial.
(c) Photos of the artists.
(d) Information about the church and other venues being used, or the district.

(C) *IDEAL CONTENTS*

All of (A) and as much of (B) as applicable or possible.
There is, of course nothing to stop you also having separate programmes for each concert, if they can be afforded. In this event their contents as appropriate to each concert should include: (e), (f), (g), (h), (i), (j), (k), (l) and (m) from Section A.

APPENDIX 10

Contents of Single, Independent Concert Programme-Brochures

(A) *ESSENTIAL CONTENTS*

(a)   Venue, time, date of concert if not on cover.
(b)   If a charity concert, include information about the charity and its address.
(c)   Artist/s' biographical notes, however brief.
(d)   Acknowledgement if artists are giving their services free.
(e)   Works to be performed, movements, composer and composer's dates.
(f)   Notes on the works.
(g)   Indication of interval, its duration, if refreshments available.
(h)   Acknowledgement of RAA/SAC assistance (if any) as required.
(i)   Acknowledgement of any other sponsorship or assistance.
(j)   Warning about Tape Recording of concert.
(k)   Name of promoter.

(B) *OPTIONAL CONTENTS*

Any of the following can be added to the above.
(a)   Fuller biographical notes.
(b)   Photos of the artists.
(c)   If charity concert, fuller notes on this and photos to do with the charity, etc.
(d)   Advertisements to offset costs.

(C) *IDEAL CONTENTS*

As appropriate, all of (A) and as much of (B) as possible.

APPENDIX 11

Guidance on Copyright

It is difficult and dangerous to try and make a generalized definition of copyright but the following statements give a rough idea of the concept:

1. Copyright exists in a musical work for the life of the composer and for 50 years after his death. It is worth noting that this applies not only to a composer, but also to an arranger, a collector of folk songs and an editor, as well as an author or translator of words of vocal music. More than one of these people may be involved in any given piece of music.
2. In addition to the copyright in the music itself, there is also a separate copyright in the graphic image of the publication.
3. If a work is not published or performed in public in a composer's lifetime, then copyright will arise when it is published or performed in public and last for 50 years from that date.

Whenever a musical work is within copyright one may not:

1. reproduce the work, or any part of it
2. publish it
3. perform it in public
4. make a recording of it
5. make any adaptation or arrangement of it
6. broadcast it

without the express permission of the copyright holder, which generally involves payment of a royalty.

Contacting the copyright holder(s) each time one wished to perform a copyright work would be very time-consuming, but one is enabled to perform most of the world's copyright music through the services of the Performing Right Society, which acts on behalf of composers, authors and publishers and which provides permission for the public performance for most types of musical work, dramatic works under most circumstances being the chief exception.'

(By kind permission of Mr Jonson Dyer and the NFMS).

APPENDIX 12

Artists' Agents

A full list of artists' agents can be found in the British Music Year Book, available in most Public Libraries. The following are especially helpful to Music Clubs and organizers of local musical events.

AIM (Artists International Management) Ltd., 5 Regent's Pk. Rd., London NW1 7TL (tel: 01 485 1009/1070)

Anderson (Helen) Musical Management, 66 Cromwell Av., London N6 5HQ (tel: 01 340 1616)

Douglas (Basil) Ltd., 8 St. George's Terr., Regent's Pk. Rd., London NW1 8JX (tel: 01 722 7142)

Graham (Barbara) Management, 35 Northwick Pk. Rd., Harrow, Middx. HA1 2NY (tel: 01 427 3394)

HHH Ltd. Concert Agency, 5 Draycott Pl., London SW3 2SF (tel: 01 584 3638)

Holt (Harold) Ltd., 134 Wigmore St., London W1H 0DJ (tel: 01 935 2331)

Ibbs & Tillett, 450–452 Edgware Rd., London W2 1EG (tel: 01 262 2864)

Ingpen & Williams Ltd., 14 Kensington Ct., London W8 5DN (tel: 01 937 5158/9)

Jennings (Helen) Concert Agency, 60 Paddington St., London W1M 3RR (tel: 01 935 2437/6819)

Koos (G. de), 416 Kings Rd., London SW10 0LJ (tel: 01 584 5849/3300)

London Artists Ltd., 124 Wigmore St., London W1H 0AX (tel: 01 486 4027/8)

Music & Musicians Artists' Management, Quinville Ho., Silsoe Rd., Maulden, Bedford MK45 2AZ (tel: 0525 402168)

New Era International Concerts, 16 Lauriston Rd., London SW19 4TQ (tel: 01 946 0467)

Nina Kaye Management, 48 Morton Street, London SW1V 2PB (tel: 01 834 1347)

Sheila Cooper Concert Artists Ltd., Elton Lodge, 13 Raynham Ave., Didsbury, Manchester M20 0BW (tel: 061 434 3103)

Tower Music, 125 Tottenham Court Rd., London W1P 9HN (tel: 01 387 4206–7/2082)

Notes on the Storage and Removal of Grand and Upright Pianos

(by kind permission of the Scottish Arts Council, from their publication *The Concert Piano in Scotland*)

STORAGE

1. Pianos should be stored in a cool, dry atmosphere with a relative humidity factor of between 42% and 55% and a temperature range of 62° to 72° Fahrenheit. Great care should be taken that the instrument is not stored:
   (a) against a radiator
   (b) against a wall that has a radiator on the other side
   (c) in direct sunlight which, even in winter can cause the temperature in a room to soar.
2. Various humidifiers and piano heaters (damp-chasers) are available to maintain stable atmospheric conditions. A piano technician should be consulted as to their use.
3. A properly made cover should be purchased to fit the piano.
4. If the instrument has to be stored for a long period it should be examined every six months to ensure that the felt has not been damaged by infestation by moth.
5. It is preferable to store a grand piano on its legs but, to save space, it may sometimes be stored on its side. In this case, a shoe or skid should be used. It is strapped to the straight side of the piano, the base leg is removed, the piano is turned on its side and the other legs and pedal removed.
6. If a grand piano is to be stored on its side it is sometimes advisable to remove the action first. This would depend on circumstances, storage time etc. but is certainly recommended for long term storage. The removal and replacing of the action should only be undertaken by a tuner/technician. The action, if removed, should be stored flat in a safe place and covered.

REMOVAL

Uprights
1. Special castors with rubber tyres can be fitted to upright pianos to enable them to be moved easily over a smooth floor. Great care should be taken, however, when moving the piano that it is not pushed over. One person at each end and one supporting the back should be sufficient to ensure that it does not happen.
2. If an upright piano has to be moved upstairs, walking girths of different lengths are

used. These go round the bottom of the piano and around the removers' shoulders who then carry the piano upstairs—a job for the expert.

Grands
1. When a grand piano has to be moved over a smooth floor at least four operators should surround the piano and as much weight as possible should be taken off the castors while it is being moved. This will avoid straining the legs.
2. If a grand has to be moved constantly it can be fitted with a trolley frame. This is a supporting triangle fixed between the legs which prevents them being strained.
3. When a grand has to be moved onto a low platform this should be managed satisfactorily if enough people are available and care is taken. However, if the piano has to be moved onto a high platform or upstairs an expert remover should be consulted. The instrument will probably have to be turned on its side into a shoe or skid and lifted with the use of a harness.

An expert piano remover is someone of intelligence rather than strength who has gained his experience from working along with others of experience. Contrary to popular belief, if a piano is carefully moved no harm should come to it.

APPENDIX 14

A Case History

Woking Music Club, which I joined at the start of its 1973–74 season, is an example of a once flourishing club going into an apparently fatal decline and then being wrested back to the rude health it now enjoys.

Founded in 1923, membership, which was 312 in its first season, rose to and stood at 500 until the early sixties when it began to drop, until by the end of that decade it was only just scraping through each season. Blame was laid on the new London South Bank complex of concert halls (only 30 minutes away by train), television and hi-fi with which the amenity-lacking venues used by the club could not compete. Most of the committee wanted to wind the club up but a few, desperately keen to continue the good work of bringing music to Woking, on learning that there was still £100 in the bank, took over and battled on. For on the horizon was one bright star. If the club could be kept alive until the completion of the town's new Centre Halls it might be saved by using either the new Theatre (capacity 250) or the Main Hall (capacity 598).

Membership continued to drop, the concerts which could be afforded offering no competition with London. Also, keen, determined and dedicated though the tenacious few were, they were not in the position to give a lot of time to the fieldwork so vital to the recruiting of members and inspiring members to do likewise, added to which publicity was almost non-existent. It was only by the skin of its teeth that the club survived until the new halls could be used. It was felt that if, after the first season in them, the club had not made good, that would be the end. Membership was then hovering around 100.

The first concert was a mistake—a recital of French songs—fine for slipping between two popular concerts but not as an opener for a first season in a new venue or for any season, for that matter! The theatre was half empty and ruin faced us. Some were for winding the club up. The rest of us were not, for we were contracted to employ a number of young international artists dependent on our kind of engagements. We went doggedly on and just succeeded, thanks to the council's meeting half the piano hire costs, an NFMS windfall of £50 on top of their guarantee, a tremendous amount of fieldwork in recruiting new members, selling non-member tickets and stepping up what was totally inadequate publicity, PR work and use of the personal approach. Membership rose to 150.

We risked a generally more ambitious programme for the following season (see page 109), boosted publicity by the use of our first interim leaflet of advance news which paid off well. I also obtained sponsorship to cover, with the SEAA's Grant in Aid, the cost of piano and harpsichord hire. Membership rose to 200, non-member ticket sales soared and we ended that season not needing our NFMS guarantee! We had broken out of the vicious circle *and* grown out of the theatre, having used the main hall for two of that season's concerts. Since then we have always used the Main Hall.

History was made during our 1977–78 season with the first ever BBC recording of a

WMC concert: Maureen Smith (violin), Keith Swallow (piano). That season also saw the premier of Alan Bush's new song-cycle *Woman's Life*, written for the soprano, Sylvia Eaves, whom Dr Bush accompanied. Both these concerts earned us considerably increased guarantees and grants. Concert programme covers, paid for by sales of advertising space were introduced during this season. Membership rose to 256, sale of non-member tickets rose well and sponsorship for hire of pianos was maintained and promised for the following season. Members' Evenings and the AGM were so well attended, that small halls instead of members' homes have since had to be used. It was also decided to increase our main concerts from five to six or more per season.

The season 1978–79 included our first ever commission (a piano piece by Michael Graubart), Grant Aid and Guarantees were again increased and SEAA covered the commission fee. Membership reached 297, though the appalling winter and flu epidemic kept the sale of non-member tickets down to the previous season's level. During this season I went all out for and obtained sponsorship from British American Tobacco (U.K. & Export) Ltd. to allow us to promote a small chamber orchestra, the first since 1963, to open our 1979–80 season, and from Johnson Wax Arts Foundation to allow us to promote a Young Artists' Concert for each of the next three seasons, as well as continuing their generous help towards piano hire costs. Even greater interest was engendered in this season's programme by the stimulus of an exhibition of photos of all the artists taking part, mounted at intervals in various parts of the town and at concerts. Membership rose to 360 of which 80 were juniors. The orchestral concert was a sell-out and attendances over our six main concerts averaged 466.2.

By offering yet another ambitious and attractive programme for 1980–81, and a 15% discount for all adults joining before 30th June 1980 we had some £3,000 earning interest in our deposit account for several months before the start of the season, by which time the membership had risen to 452. Thanks to substantial sponsorship by Audi GB/Colborne Garages Ltd of Ripley, we were able to continue our policy of opening the season with a chamber orchestra and so give an outstanding young artist the chance to work as soloist with a professional orchestra. Our subscription covers the cost of admission to all our concerts and is reduced pro rata after each of them.

Our members come from all walks of life and are of all ages. Especially heartwarming is the fact that we are winning back many who left in the '60s due to their 'dissatisfaction with the club and fall-off in the standard of concerts'. Furthermore those who have returned encourage others to do so. Indeed, nearly everyone who joins is now spreading the word with a splendid snowballing effect. There is a growing interest and support in the furthering of outstanding young artists' careers, and at last we are going a long way towards playing our roles on both sides of the platform, as it were, while endeavouring to do even better. And to that end, in order to obtain maximum financial benefit we have become a Registered Charity.

In 1983–84 we celebrate our Diamond Jubilee. Plans are already afoot to stir up the whole town for enough sponsorship to allow us to promote a season of the most ambitious concerts yet, not forgetting outstanding young artists and a possible commission to commemorate our 60th birthday by which time membership should be at least 600.

Could we have achieved such a comeback without the new venue? Given the know-how, drive, dedication, initiative and plenty of time to devote to the project, I believe that it would have been possible. The new halls have helped tremendously, but are by no means ideal for the performance of music. The acoustics are too dry and our present project under way is to do something about this. We also have to contend with what can be an uncomfortable build-up of body heat because the noisy heating and air conditioning plants have to be off during performances. On the other hand the hall management and staff co-operation is excellent, seating comfortable, cloakrooms good, bars and coffee lounge well run.

But the new venue is far from being the entire reason for our success. Because, as I cannot emphasise enough, you can have the plushiest, most interesting of venues, the most attractive of programmes, but if no one knows about them or what goes on in them you will get nowhere. One way and another, and with respect, I believe that many clubs, my own included, need never have run into trouble if there had been a different approach to their running and image projection. And what goes for the clubs goes for any amateur concert-promoting project.

WOKING MUSIC CLUB

CONCERTS AND AVERAGE ATTENDANCES EACH SEASON SINCE MOVING INTO CENTRE HALLS WOKING

T = Concerts in Rhoda McGaw Theatre, Centre Halls (capacity 250)
MH = Concerts in Main Hall (capacity 598)

1975–1976 (Fifty-Second Season) Average Attendance 169.6

Oct.	(T)	Carole Rosen (mezzo-sop.), Paul Hamburger (piano) *The Art of French Song:* Berlioz, Duparc, Fauré, Ravel, Debussy
Nov.	(T)	Roll Trio. Michael Roll (piano), Mayumi Fujikawa (violin), Richard Markson ('cello) Mendelssohn, Brahms, Schubert
Jan.	(T)	Zephyr Wind/Piano Quintet Danzi, Lees, Hindemith, Schuller, Poulenc
Feb.	(T)	Maureen Smith (violin), Keith Swallow (piano) Elgar, Beethoven, Saint-Saëns
Mar.	(T)	Myung-Whun Chung (piano) Haydn, Beethoven, Berg, Debussy, Chopin

1976–1977 (Fifty-Third Season) Average Attendance 255.2

Oct.	(MH)	John Lill (piano) Haydn, Beethoven, Chopin, Prokofiev
Nov.	(MH)	Richard Hickox Orchestra (small group). Directed from harpsichord by Richard Hickox. Soloist: Simon Standage (violin) Purcell, Bach, Pachelbel, Bononcini
Jan.	(T)	Ian Partridge (tenor), Jennifer Partridge (piano) Britten, Beethoven, Purcell, Brahms
Feb.	(T)	Occasional Wind Players (semi-professional), (2nd appearance for club). Directed by Geoffrey Hartley Mozart, Gabrieli, Lewis Jones, Uhl, Auric
Mar.	(T)	Jack Brymer (clarinet), Gwen Rolph (piano). Lecture Recital Weber, Finzi, Tartini (Audience overflowed onto platform. Decided to use MH for all future main concerts.)

1977–1978 (Fifty-Fourth Season) Average Attendance 343.4

Oct.	(MH)	Gabrieli String Quartet (3rd appearance for club) Dvorak, Shostakovich, Beethoven
Nov.	(MH)	Maureen Smith (violin), Keith Swallow (piano). *Recital recorded by BBC* Handel, Prokofiev, Hindemith, Beethoven
Jan.	(MH)	Leon Goossens (oboe) (2nd appearance for club) Lecture Recital

109

Feb.	(MH)	Sylvia Eaves (sop.), Dr Alan Bush (composer/piano)

Feb. (MH) Sylvia Eaves (sop.), Dr Alan Bush (composer/piano)
Premier of *Woman's Life,* song-cycle for soprano and piano, words by Nancy Bush, music by Alan Bush; songs by Purcell, Michael Head, Handel

Mar. (MH) Peter Katin (piano) (2nd appearance for club)
Bach, Schumann, Schubert, Katin, Chopin

1978–1979 (Fifty-Fifth Season) Average Attendance 339 (6 concerts)

Sept. (MH) Radu Lupu (piano)
All Schubert evening

Oct. (MH) Dame Isobel Baillie (sop.) at least 4th visit to club, John Grierson (piano)
Lecture Recital

Nov. (MH) Melos Ensemble of London (wind/piano Quintet)
Stamitz, Poulenc, Lennox Berkeley, Mozart

Jan. (MH) Wheatley Ensemble (string sextet)
Bach, Mozart, Tchaikovsky

Feb. (MH) Kathron Sturrock (piano)
Mozart, Britten, Chopin and specially commissioned work by Michael Graubart

Mar. (MH) Teresa Cahill (sop.), Roger Vignoles (piano)
Schubert, Fauré, Strauss, Handel

1979–1980 (Fifty-Sixth Season) Average Attendance 466.2 (6 concerts)

Oct. (MH) Grand Opening Concert sponsored by BAT (U.K. & Export) Ltd. London Mozart Players. Conductor: Harry Blech. Soloist: Maureen Smith (violin)
Handel, Mozart violin concerto, Elgar, Haydn
(This concert sold out)

Nov. (MH) Julian Lloyd Webber ('cello), Simon Nicholls (piano)
Vivaldi, John Ireland, Brahms
(This nearly sold out)

Dec. (MH) Sylvia Kersenbaum (piano)
Handel/Brahms, Schumann, Berg, Glinka/Balakirev, Liszt

Jan. (MH) 'The Songmakers' Almanac': Susan Dennis (sop.), Richard Jackson (bar.), Graham Johnson (piano). Theme *The Ruling Passions:* Wolf, Poulenc, Coward, Mozart, Brahms

Feb. (MH) The 1st Johnson Wax Arts Foundation 'Young Artists' Concert'
The Deakin Piano Trio
Ravel, Brahms, Beethoven

Mar. (MH) Howard Shelley (piano) (2nd appearance for club)
Haydn, Mussorgsky, Michael Berkeley, Chopin, Brough

1980–1981 (Fifty-Seventh Season) Average Attendance 501 over 1st three concerts

Oct. (MH) Grand Opening Concert sponsored by Audi GB/Colborne Garages Ltd. City of London Sinfonia. Conductor: Richard

Hickox. Soloist: David Campbell (clarinet)
Schubert, Mozart Clarinet Concerto, Tippett, Haydn
(Nearly sold out)

Nov. (MH) 2nd Johnson Wax Arts Foundation 'Young Artists' Concert'
Alison Truefitt (mezzo-sop.), Clara Taylor (piano), Hanson
String Quartet, in shared evening as at their Purcell Room
debut
Haydn Quartet, Songs by Poulenc, Granados, Barber with piano,
Butterworth with quartet, Chausson with piano quintet and
Elgar's piano quintet

Dec. (MH) *An Evening with Ian Wallace* (bass-bar.), Mary Nash (piano)
(Sold out)

Jan. (MH) Two Prize Winners of Leeds 1980 National Competition for
Musicians
Peter Savidge (bass-bar.), 2nd prize, David Owen-Norris (piano)
accompanists' prize
Songs by Purcell, Schubert, Fauré, Mozart, Finzi, Warlock,
Vaughan Williams. Piano works by Poulenc and Bax

Feb. (MH) Sheba Sound. Wind/Harpsichord Ensemble
Handel, Couperin, Arne, Martinu, Langford, Beethoven, Beatles/
Tony Hymas

Mar. (MH) Moura Lympany (piano), Franck, Haydn, Beethoven, Liszt

MEMBERS' EVENINGS AND EVENTS SINCE 1975

PH = Private House.   HH = Hired Hall

1975–1976 *Average Attendance 25*

Feb. (PH) Illustrated talk *Verdi—Why I am an Enthusiast*, W. Llewelyn,
Director of Music, Charterhouse

April (PH) *Members' Concert* by members for members

1976–1977 *Average Attendance 44*

Dec. (PH) *A Musical Evening* by Mrs Davina Marshall (prof. violin), husband
Peter (piano), son David ('cello), daughter Helen (piano and
clarinet)

April (PH) The Chanticleer Singers of Radlett

1977–1978 *Average Attendance 62*

Nov. (PH) Illustrated talk, *Historic Performances on Record—a Miscellany*
by Lionel Markson

April (PH) *Members' Concert* by members for members

1978–1979 *Average Attendance 95*

Oct. (HH) Illustrated talk *The Life of Kathleen Ferrier* by Esmé Parsons
Mar. (HH) Demonstration concert by London Suzuki Group

111

Nov.	(HH)	Alison Truefitt (mezzo-sop.) accompanied by Clara Taylor (piano) talked about building her career and sang works she performed two days later at her Purcell Room debut shared with the Hanson String quartet
April	(HH)	*Members' Concert* by members for members
July		Outing to the Festival of English Music at South Hill Arts Centre, Bracknell, some 50 members attended

1980–1981

Oct.	(HH)	Gilbert & Sullivan Evening by members and friends of Walton & Weybridge Operatic Society. Attendance 102
Nov.		Outing to piano recital by Howard Shelley in the Q.E.H. South Bank (46 came)
Feb.	(HH)	*Reminiscences of an Impresario* Wilfrid Van Wyck, preceded by buffet supper
Mar.	(HH)	*Concert* by professional members of the club. Frances Dodd (piano). Clive McCombie (bass-bar.), acc. Nina Brough (piano), Leonard Paice (flute), acc. Judith Lambden (piano)
April	(HH)	*Illustrated Talk* by conductor Vernon Handley

112

BIBLIOGRAPHY

REFERENCE BOOKS & PACKS

Arts Council Annual Report
A Simple Guide to Committee Procedure by Eleanor O. Lambourne (Allen & Unwin)
British Music Year Book (Bowker)
Directory of Grant Making Trusts
Fund-Raising by Hilary Blume (Routlege & Kegan Paul)
Fund-Raising by Charities (National Council of Social Service, London)
Fund-Raising Handbook by Redmond Mullins (Mowbrays 1976)
Groves Dictionary of Music & Musicians
Incorporated Society of Musicians' Professional Register of Artists
International Who's Who in Music
Larousse Encyclopedia of Music
Manual of Public Relations by Bowman & Ellis
Marketing the Arts by Keith Diggle: available from the *Arts & Related Studies* at City University, St. John's St., London EC1V 4PB
Music Matters: available from the *Standing Conference for Amateur Music* at 26 Bedford Square, London WC1B 3HU (This is a check list for local music groups with suggestions on how to make use of available resources etc.)
Music Publishers' catalogues giving instrumentation and duration of works
National Federation of Music Societies' Register of Members & Handbook
New Musical Companion (Gollancz)
Oxford Companion of Music (Scholes)
Raising Money for the Arts available from the *Directory of Social Change*, 9 Mansfield Place, London NW3.

Raising Money from Government
Raising Money from Industry
Raising Money from Trusts
Raising Money through Special Events
}
Information packs containing loose-leaf sheets of edited transcripts of a series of fund-raising seminars organized by the *Directory of Social Change* from whom available. Reduced rates for charitable organizations.

The Musician's Survival Kit by Leonard Pearcey (Barry & Jenkins)
The Concert Piano in Scotland a report to the Scottish Arts Council from whom it is available (see Appendix 13)
Training and Careers for Professional Musicians by Gerald MacDonald (Gresham Books)

WEEKLIES, PERIODICALS & DAILIES

Classical Music
The Composer
The Gramophone
Musical Opinion
Musical Times

Music Week
Music in Wales
The Strad
Music Sections in some County Magazines
Regional Arts Associations' Publications

Index